What people are

Ancient Teachings fo   ..... Times

Peta Morton has done a marvelous job of extracting the gold from ancient spiritual wisdom to help you improve your quality of life. I wish that I had found her writing at the beginning of my personal journey. It would have shortened my arrival time.
Mark Certo (thetriadmind.com), creator of *The Triad Mind*, producer, former recording engineer for the Monroe Institute

This engaging and superbly written book is part spiritual discourse, part practical handbook for an awakened life, and succeeds in illuminating every hidden reach of our being. Peta Morton brilliantly weaves together the wisdom of ancient spiritual traditions with a refreshingly practical and grounded approach to what it really means to be human.

An essential guide to living an awakened, more conscious life, drawing on the ancient wisdom traditions and making them relevant for our technology-driven times. This thoroughly researched and superbly written book connects the dots across the ages, making the arcane wisdom of the sages and the mystics accessible and relevant to the modern reader, providing essential insights and practical guidance so we can live our best possible lives.
Nick Day (conscious-pictures.com/consciousness-central), award-winning filmmaker and presenter of *Consciousness Central TV*

Beautifully written, almost poetic, from a master teacher who has both distilled and synthesized the gifts of philosophy and science to provide a clear doorway to personal cultivation.
Karen Adams, Lic. Ac., Dipl. Ac., BS, BA (Hons), acupuncturist specializing in personal, combat and critical incident trauma

In this gloriously simple book Peta shows that facing our fears doesn't have to be scary. Instead she encourages us to be curious and open-minded, showing up as who we really are and living fun, full and authentic lives.

Andrew Martin (andrewmartin.energy), host of international radio show *A Life Untethered*, energy intuitive, sound healer and spiritual guide

A simple guide to living a happy life. Wonderful! Warm, wise and thought-provoking.

Maurizio Benazzo, filmmaker and co-founder of the *Science and Nonduality Conference (SAND)*

Ancient Teachings for Modern Times is a book I shall not only read more than once but also recommend to my friends and students in the philosophical, esoteric and psychological communities. From the correlations between cultures of expressions for life force to alchemy, breathing techniques and the nature of emotion: the insights of Peta Morton reflect the dynamics of what I have been teaching for more than twenty-seven years. The practical steps outlined in 'Experience' are easy to follow and they work! If you have an interest in self-understanding or are seeking tools to assist yourself or others in life, please read this book.

David Charles Rowan, MA Msc. (davidrowan.co.uk), astrologer, psychologist, author

Such a beautifully written book with such complexity I have to keep stopping to digest it. It is truly a work of art.

Kothai Kanthan, Managing Editor, *Resonant Content*

In Ancient Teachings for Modern Times, Peta Morton elegantly weaves together practical wisdom from a diverse array of traditions to provide a 'one stop shop' for anyone interested in personal development and well-being. This synthesis of

important teachings and modalities – ranging from the power of
breathing, thoughts, gratitude, and beyond – has the potential to
shift the reader's perspective and clears the path for a happier,
more peaceful life.

Mark Gober (markgober.com), #1 bestselling author of *An End
to Upside Down Thinking*, Director of Corporate Relations at Dr.
Erwin Lazlo's Institute of New Paradigm Research

In this book, Peta Morton makes a brave effort in bridging
the gap between disciplines. Her work offers an unbiased
overview of the fundamental insights about the nature of the
human experience. In the spirit of Aldous Huxley's perennial
philosophy, she crosses the centuries and provides the reader
with a deep intercultural fresco of mystical experience.

Riccardo Manzotti PhD., (consciousness.it), Professor of
Philosophy at IULM University of Milan, Fulbright Visiting
Scholar at MIT, author of *The Spread Mind* and 50 papers on
consciousness, artificial intelligence, machine consciousness and
perception

In *Ancient Teachings for Modern Times*, Peta Morton takes the
reader wading easily into subjects previously considered too
esoteric: metaphysics and the interconnectedness of life. She
offers scientific validation for what most people considered
mysterious: the vibrations of life, how thoughts matter (literally!),
and most of all, her book could be considered required reading
as a guide to life itself.

Alice Langholt, M.MSc. (reikiawakening.com), author of
*Practical Reiki: for balance, well-being, and vibrant health. A guide to
a simple, revolutionary energy healing method*

By offering a rich mix of theories, thoughts, traditions,
religions and practical examples, Peta illustrates clearly how
interconnected, boundless and timeless we are: how we are all

but one. A beautifully-written piece offering greater meaning, joy and fulfilment to the lives of the reader. It's a book anyone could pick up and read, spiritual knowledge, pathway or not.
Jacqueline Cripps (jacquelinecripps.com), Grad Dip. Psych (Hons), B. Social Sc., author of *#WTF is happening with my life? A Guide To Getting Your Sh*t Together*, speaker, mentor, certified clinical trauma practitioner, art therapist

This book's insights and practical wisdom will be an eye opener and provide support for anyone needing a nudge in the right direction.
Natasha Hoffman (natashahoffmanbooks.com), author of *Let the Standing Stones Speak*, artist, intuitive healer

Packed full of information but delivered in a way that is easy to digest, with gentle humor and love, and not preachy at all. It flows effortlessly and makes stepping up to the game of becoming a worthwhile human being seem achievable.
Lucy Hodges (Lucy Hodges Coaching), author of *Mandalas for the Soul*, healer, creative life coach

In this great work Peta Morton states 'nothing herein is new'. What is new and refreshing is her deeply insightful perspective and clear illustrations of the vast body of spiritual works left to us by our favorite masters. Using science, art, philosophy, chemistry, physics and great love, she challenges us to remember that we have choices: to learn what the Ancient Greeks and Chinese knew – how to live heart-centered lives and tune into our vibrational frequencies. As our trusted guide she takes us on a breathtakingly beautiful journey through the mechanics of the links between mind and matter. In this simple rendering of complex theories she shows us how, by making small but essentially important and tangible adjustments, we can change the world for the better. This little book is a very timely treasure

and a must read for people of all ages!
Sybil Kleinmichel (Sycheck Foundation), life coach and
executive director of Sycheck Foundation

A lucid, concise approach to holistic healing.
Parag Pattani (Parag's Reiki Hut), international Reiki master

Peta has synthesized the wisdom of the ages in her new book
blending ancient teachings, innate intelligence and modern
science to help the reader move toward spiritual maturity.
I was delighted to discover our books' many shared inspirations,
as well as a rich cache of numerous others, presented in a direct
and considered manner. Pick up this book, share it with your
circle, and discover new ways to be more conscious of what you
throw into the river of your life.
Dielle Ciesco (dielleciesco.com), author of *The Unknown Mother:
A Magical Walk with the Goddess of Sound* and *Your True Voice:
Tools to Embrace a Fully-Expressed Life*

Amazing book – so many insights, so easy to read, not too much
at a time.
Hamilton Hill, author and artist

Ancient Teachings for Modern Times

The way to a rich and deeply
satisfying life

Ancient Teachings for Modern Times

The way to a rich and deeply
satisfying life

Peta Morton

BOOKS

Winchester, UK
Washington, USA

JOHN HUNT PUBLISHING

First published by O-Books, 2019
O-Books is an imprint of John Hunt Publishing Ltd., 3 East St., Alresford,
Hampshire SO24 9EE, UK
office@jhpbooks.com
www.johnhuntpublishing.com
www.o-books.com

For distributor details and how to order please visit the 'Ordering' section on our website.

ISBN: 978 1 78904 083 8
978 1 78904 242 9 (ebook)
Library of Congress Control Number: 2018957144

A CIP catalogue record for this book is available from the British Library.

Design: Stuart Davies

UK: Printed and bound by CPI Group (UK) Ltd, Croydon, CR0 4YY
US: Printed and bound by Thomson-Shore, 7300 West Joy Road, Dexter, MI 48130

We operate a distinctive and ethical publishing philosophy in all areas of our business, from our global network of authors to production and worldwide distribution.

Contents

Preface   1
How to Use This Book   3

Chapter 1: Vibrational You   4
Chapter 2: The Breath of Life   23
Chapter 3: Thoughts Are Things   39
Chapter 4: Limiting Beliefs   57
Chapter 5: The Word   71
Chapter 6: Emotion   84
Chapter 7: Handing It Over   117
Chapter 8: The Wee Small Hours   124
Chapter 9: Appreciation   130
Chapter 10: Integrity   139
Chapter 11: Taking Responsibility   146
Chapter 12: Taking Action   157
Chapter 13: The Rhythm of Life   165
Chapter 14: Community   183

Bibliography   212
Note from the Author   225

This book is dedicated, with profound gratitude, to Laure-Anne Coulombier, to Zaida Catalán and to Jill Saward, who continue to inspire and uplift. They did not waste a second.

Theologians may quarrel, but the mystics of this world speak the same language.
– **Meister Eckhart**

Nothing in this book is new.

Acknowledgements

To Karl, Ellie and George, thank you for all the times I said, "Shhh!! I'm writing."

I love you.

Preface

This is the book that I would like to have been given when I started my own journey. It is not a definitive guide. Indeed, many of the topics I have touched upon here have had entire books written about them in their own right. This book will show you that living well doesn't have to be complicated. It can be as simple as breathing and being. The easy techniques I have shared here can be practiced by anybody, no matter what their age, gender, background or experience.

I encourage you not to accept anything written here on face value. Don't just take my word for it. This book is merely a guide, a signpost. Test things out for yourself. *You* are the best expert on what resonates with you, so give yourself permission to make your own mind up whether there is any validity in these words or not. We are all unique. We each experience life differently, through our own filters and from our own perspectives. What is an amazing technique for one person may be bewildering for another and a complete nonevent for someone else. Explore how things feel for you. Take what works best, dismiss or develop the things that don't. Be childlike, have fun, be playful. Experiment and don't be afraid to try things out, adapt these ideas and tweak them so that they feel comfortable and fit effortlessly into your life. You cannot go wrong. Share what you discover.

At this moment in time we understand life primarily from a linear perspective. As we become increasingly aware of the nature of our multidimensionality then our understanding is likely to evolve. So hold what you read here loosely. Very loosely.

The straightforward, manageable practices within these pages have been shown time and time again to improve well-being and health, enhancing intuition and peace of mind. They are not complex. There is no fuss. No rigmarole. You don't need to study for years and years to see results. It's not essential to understand the ins and outs of how these methods work in order for them to be effective, although these words may prompt further study of some of the subject matter. They may inspire a deeper, more thorough, exploration of the inner self. By incorporating even a few of the concepts shared in this book into your life you will open a door to a wealth of possibilities.

Be ready for your world to transform in profound and wonderful ways.

Peta Morton

How to Use This Book

This book is intended to be used in two different ways. You may choose to read it from cover to cover, in the traditional way, or you may simply choose to open it to a page at random. Either way, if you are reading with an open and questioning mind the right words will find you.

Chapter 1

Vibrational You

In the beginning
There was neither existence nor non-existence,
All this world was unmanifest energy...
– **Nasadiya Sukta (The Hymn of Creation), the Rig Veda**

Who are you really? *What* are you? Consider this for a moment. Your physical body is constructed from a variety of chemical elements, assembled in such a way as to form molecules, cells, blood, bones, organs, teeth, hair. A staggeringly large number of atoms – an estimated seven billion billion billion, which is a number almost too vast to contemplate – cooperate in accordance with Natural laws to produce the physical representation that you describe as 'you'. You are made from the very same basic building blocks of life that permeate our entire galaxy, bound together in complex ways to form intricately detailed structures. Within a period of seven years or so, every single one of the atoms in your body will be replaced. You will get a haircut and trim your nails and they will regrow. Scabs will form over open wounds, only to fall, replaced by fresh new skin. Your blood will be replenished. Your organs will regenerate. You are not the same person you were even a few moments ago.

Clearly, your physical form is nothing like the one that gasped for air as you first entered this world. You are a very different configuration of molecules today to the one that resembled that toddler making mud pies. You probably don't appear much like the pouting adolescent you once used to, trying to look cool in front of your friends, nor the version of you that eases into old age. You certainly don't look like the you that might one day lie still beneath the ground, or be scattered to the four winds many years from now. Yet despite all these changes you retain a sense of self. Even following the amputation of multiple limbs you would feel no less you. You know you are still the same person, despite the physical transformation that is constantly taking place. Who are you then, if you are not just the sum of your physical parts? If you being you is not dependent upon a collection of physical components, then you must surely be comprised of aspects and attributes that are nonphysical.

You are a collection of thoughts and experiences and the information you have accumulated about them, a bundle of beliefs, memories and emotions. You are the stories you tell yourself. A master translator of frequency and vibration, you are a wondrous synthesizer of life. Your bodily instrument is a musical marvel, constantly generating a glorious spectrum of sound, both audible and inaudible, combining electrical signals of different frequencies. You are simultaneously a transmitter, receiver and interpreter of data, like some magnificent router that is always connected, ever in intimate relationship to all that exists. You are an array of ordered photons, particles and waves of light. You are a powerful and indestructible force. Above all, you are a process, ongoing, never finished, an integral part of life seeking to experience itself.

We are vibrational beings. Every thought, every emotion, every sound, every smell, every color that we are capable of perceiving is merely our interpretation of vibration.

If you want to find the secrets of the Universe, think in terms of energy, frequency and vibration.
– Nikola Tesla

We see, smell and feel things because they vibrate. We hear sound because of changes of air pressure, vibrating at differing speeds within our eardrums. Each and every vibration has its own unique signature and specific frequency.

Today's scientists are finding that at the most minute scale we are capable of studying – the quarks and leptons of quantum physics – there is very little, if anything, that is substantial about the things that appear in our material world. Everything that exists within this visible galaxy is made of energetic particles in motion in space, energy vibrating at different rates. A steel girder might appear extremely solid and stable, but this is just a very powerful illusion. Matter is mind-bogglingly empty. Within the structure of all matter are a vast number of subatomic particles, each seemingly vibrating and randomly popping in and out of existence, behaving in accordance with the laws of nature that scientists have dubbed 'quantum mechanics', in ways that we are still grappling to understand. If we examine any solid object under a powerful microscope we will find that only around 0.1 percent is made of ephemeral subatomic particles, which change from matter to waveform depending upon how we observe them. These changes pose a huge challenge for scientists as, for the time being at least, it makes measurement impossible. The solidity of this remaining 0.1 percent may well be called into question as our technology evolves and we develop instruments capable of scrutinizing the tiniest of tiny things even more closely. It seems increasingly likely that these subatomic entities are just oscillations, without any solidity at all.

What's left is mere excitations of force fields.
– **Dr. Jude Currivan**

Solid matter is simply energy that is more readily perceived. When things vibrate more quickly they become less visible to most people's limited range of perception, even though they still exist. The extent to which they are audible changes. A good example of this is the humble electric fan. When it is still or moving slowly it is very easy to see and it appears as a solid object. Yet if we increase the speed at which the fan rotates it becomes blurred, and if we turn the speed up really fast it becomes transparent and almost disappears from view.

It's said that if we were able to remove the space from our bodies, the whole of our compacted humanity could be squeezed into an area the size of a single cube of sugar. The remaining 99.9 percent is seemingly devoid of substance yet it oscillates with vibrational frequency, like music, teeming with potentiality. This offers much food for thought, as our ancient forebears held this primal sound to be at the origin of all material existence.

The notion of energy is so abstract that scientists have yet to define it, or agree on what it consists of. Indeed, at the time of writing science has also still to define concepts such as mind, consciousness and mental health. When Dr. Daniel J. Siegel, a pioneer in the field of interpersonal neurobiology, asked a group of 150 physicists the question "What is energy?" their collective response after many deep and insightful conversations was:

Energy is the movement from possibility to actuality.

The truth is, it is impossible to put a label on. It is something that is beyond words and labels, beyond human comprehension. It is the essence of all life and is omnipresent, sustaining everything that exists: humans, plants, animals and minerals, the water that we drink, the air that we breathe, the earth that supports us. This mysterious energy flows through every atom, from the smallest molecule to the largest planet, permeating the entire cosmos. It is formless, yet is the motivating principle via which form is organized and structured, linking spirit and substance. Imperceptible, this indefinable force is what sustains life and animates all living beings. It is what makes the sun shine and the trees and flowers grow. Since time immemorial great sages, yogis, seers and spiritual masters from every corner of our world and every conceivable culture have talked of it:

There is a force in the Universe, which, if we permit it, will flow through us and produce miraculous results.
– **Mahatma Gandhi**

It is not associated with any visible material being. It's an unseen spiritual power that radiates vibration and lifts one into harmony. This power is incomprehensible to man, yet every single living being is receiving its blessings.
– **Hawayo Takata**

We hear this benevolent, intelligent, infinite life force energy referred to by many different names:

- Qi or chi (Chinese)
- Ki (Japanese)
- Prana (Sanskrit)
- Spiritus (Latin)
- Aether or ether (Latin)
- Pneuma (Ancient Greek)
- Holy Spirit (Christian)
- Sekhem (Egyptian)
- Great Spirit (Native American)
- Gitche Manitou or Kije Manito (Algonquian)
- Wakan Tanka (Lakota)
- Mana (Polynesian)
- Lüng (Tibetan Buddhism)
- Megin (Norse)
- Rûaħ or ruach (Hebrew)
- Quintessence (Middle English)
- The fifth element

to name but a few. In scientific circles it is more likely to be discussed in the context of electromagnetic emission or photonic radiation. We can call it anything we like, but we can never be separate from it. It affects all levels of our being: physical, mental, emotional and spiritual. Since the dawn of time the great religious and spiritual texts have pointed to non-duality, telling of the interconnectedness, the oneness, of all things. All ancient philosophies have told of the ways in which this vital essence gives life to all creative thought, enabling it to manifest in our physical reality. It is an exquisite, loving, benevolent, balanced, unpolluted and harmonious state of pure consciousness in which all possibilities exist. It is our True nature.

Many things can't be seen with the naked eye, which is why we have microscopes. A great deal of vibrational information is of a frequency which is way beyond the normal range of human awareness, yet it exists nevertheless. The vast majority of people are aware of less than one percent of the electromagnetic and acoustic spectrums. The average range of human hearing includes sound frequencies between 15–20,000 Hz, or cycles per second. Outside of this range sound goes undetected by most people. Elephants, with their large ears, can pick up infra-sounds, low frequencies that to us seem inaudible. Dolphins communicate using low frequencies and make use of high frequencies for echolocation. Bats too use high frequency ultrasound to navigate. The human eye is only capable of seeing a miniscule portion of the electromagnetic spectrum, that which lies between 390 and 700 nm (a band of around 430–770 THz in frequency terms) which we refer to as 'visible light', whereas eagles see the world in vivid brilliance with far more clarity of focus. Isn't it funny how we readily accept that a dog can hear a high pitched whistle which is inaudible to most human ears? We acknowledge concepts such as radio, microwave and gamma waves, yet are often deeply skeptical of notions such as subtle energy and psychic sight.

Within this closed system that we call earth the very same water that nourished our ancestors thousands of years earlier continually shifts states, changing from liquid to ice, to cloud, to rain and to steam. The amount of space in between each particle increases or decreases in response to thermal and pressure changes, causing substances to expand and contract, to become lighter or denser and to behave in different ways. Particles that are active or 'excited' vibrate quickly and produce heat while those that are closer to stillness are cooler. The same processes are constantly occurring within the unseen world, they just pass largely unnoticed. Through movement and vibratory rates, the subtle becomes become grosser, denser, descending so as to manifest in a way which is physically visible, while that which is apparent ascends to become more ethereal in nature.

Our inward being, our essence, is comprised of very fine vibrations, whereas our outer being and the external material world we see around us are formed from gross vibrations. We often hear the finer part referred to as spirit, and the grosser part as matter. Life materializes from the stillness of the soul through greater levels of vibrational activity generated in no small measure by our thoughts and our emotions.

Experience
Light a stick of incense and watch the smoke plume rise upwards. At what point does the smoke no longer exist? Listen intently to the oscillating voice of a Tibetan singing bowl. At what point does the sound no longer exist?

At any given moment each of us is emitting our own unique vibrational tone, dependent upon what we are thinking and feeling at the time. But what determines how that tone manifests into something that can be perceived in our physical reality? The life we see around us is molded by that insubstantial, unreliable force called human will, by the decisions that we make and the actions we take. If we learn to properly manage our vibrational tone then we are much better able to experience the richness that life has to offer, rather than be enslaved by it. This is not always easy to do; it takes practice. Just as it is hard to stop a ball once it is rolling down a hill, it's not always possible to call back the events that occur once our thoughts have gained a great deal of momentum. Yet the desire to be able to regulate one's vibrational state is a valuable aspiration to hold, as it is through vibration that mastery is achieved.

Every vibration has both length and breadth, frequency and amplitude. The lower the frequency that is produced, the longer the standing wave it generates and vice versa; the higher the frequency, the shorter the standing wave. Each frequency has a musical note that is associated with it. A higher frequency sound wave corresponds to a high pitch and a lower frequency to a lower pitch.

Although it has been dimmed by manifestation, your thought, your mind, is also made of sound.
 – Hazrat Inayat Khan

Within the spectrum of visible light each frequency is related to a specific color. As the frequency gets higher so the colors change, ranging from red (low frequency) through to orange, yellow, green, blue and violet (high frequency). A vibration may be fleeting or it may last for billions of years. The vibrations of the soul are amongst the most powerful, extending far in their influence.

As particles vibrate at different rates, or frequencies, they move and behave in different ways, offering the potential for changes of state and transformation. Those in solids are compacted closely in a regular pattern, and vibrate in a fixed position, attracted and held together by strong forces called bonds. In liquids such as water or mercury they are bonded randomly, still close but in a way which allows them to move around each other, so that they are able to flow and take the shape of their container. The particles of gases such as air, helium, water vapor and chlorine are spaced further apart and are arranged in a random way. They are not bonded, so can move rapidly in all directions.

Empty your mind! Be formless, shapeless, like water. You put water into a cup, it becomes the cup. You put water into a teapot, it becomes the teapot. Water can flow, or creep or drip or crash. Be water, my friend.
– Bruce Lee

When energy is added to or subtracted from a substance its physical state changes. For example, by adding heat through kinetic energy (the energy of something in motion), molecules move and vibrate more quickly causing the strength of the bonds holding them together to decrease. When energy is decreased the process is reversed. Changes in temperature cause the light of an object to brighten or dim, sometimes quite dramatically, and they affect the pitch of sound and the speed at which it travels.

Many of those who have had mystical experiences describe feeling intense vibrations and heat in the moments immediately preceding them. To the Ancient Greeks, the original source of vital heat in every living being lies in the heart, and is intimately connected with the soul. They taught that just as the sun lies at the center of our solar system, imparting life and light to all the planets that revolve around it, so the heart is crucial to all parts of the body. Without it there can be no motion, intelligence or sensation. The Ancient Chinese were of a similar opinion, considering the heart to be the king of all organs and recognizing that all other organs will sacrifice themselves if necessary to keep the heart in balance. They held that the heart houses the *shen*, our mind, spirit and vitality, and is responsible for regulating the circulation of blood. The heart influences our mental activity, intellect, emotions, memories and conscious awareness.

Intense activity in any sphere, such as that of a stormy ocean or a violent tornado, has destructive power and the potential to destroy everything in its wake, bringing weakness and damage. Spiritual energy can be seen more like a calm sea. It is much less subject to change and destruction than matter. Oscillating like an electric current between souls, one vibration inspires changes in the vibrations of another and thus gives rise to a myriad of forms and colors. In between these two extremes lies balance, like the ebb and flow of a moderately active sea in gentle motion.

Just as every individual wave forms part of a greater oceanic whole, so all things in the galaxy are interconnected, both visibly and invisibly, through the subtle language of vibration. We each retain our own sense of identity, our own uniqueness, yet on some level we are all part of the same thing, inextricably meshed together. This 'Oneness' that is so often mentioned in esoteric belief systems around the world is not always immediately apparent in our busy day-to-day lives. Nevertheless, at a certain level of our consciousness – that which some refer to as 'super-consciousness' – this state of Oneness very much exists. This collective consciousness is like a huge database of knowledge, thoughts, feelings and experiences; one vast heart-mind that can be accessed by all of us if the right conditions are met.

Experience
Light two candles and put them side by side. Gaze at them intently in a relaxed way for a few minutes. At what point does the light emanating from one end and the light from the other begin? What colors do you see within the light?

One vibration can easily communicate its condition to another. We can all bring to mind someone yawning loudly followed by everybody in the room yawning along with them in response. Laughter, and emotions such as excitement, depression and anger are equally contagious. When someone is offended their displeasure is palpable, even if they have their back turned and speak no words. No matter how far away someone is, the vibrations of hostility are easily felt. Any disturbance ripples throughout the whole, like those of a stone thrown onto the surface of a still pond, until it eventually returns to its originator. When we live peacefully we bring serenity to the whole, and peace is returned to us. Ultimately, at the conclusion of every vibration made manifest, it is absorbed back into its originating source.

Everything in life is in perpetual motion, continually changing. Everything, including change itself. No amount of angry denial will stem the ever-evolving, restless flux and flow of the Universe. A quirk of birth, good fortune or tenacity may have provided us with a temporary sense of privilege and entitlement, but if we don't have the word humility in our vocabulary we would be wise to learn it quickly. Change is inevitable, and those who are astute accept it gladly.

If you realize that all things change there is nothing you will try to hold onto.
– **Lao Tzu**

No man ever steps in the same river twice.
– **Heraclitus**

Just as we can only pick up a particular radio station if we are tuned in to it, or watch a TV program if we have first selected the right channel, so we can only perceive the things that are of a similar vibrational frequency to us. We cannot listen to Radio One if we're tuned to Radio Four. A multitude of TV and radio stations exist, and there are many, many programs to watch, all of which are either already created or being broadcast in real time. They are just waiting for us to plug the television in, turn it on and zap the remote or push the button that takes us to the program we prefer. Many more programs are in the process of being created, or are still just a vague idea in the writer's mind. It is impossible to watch a program on a different channel unless we first change channels. Getting the best out of life can be as simple as changing vibrational frequency so that it matches the frequency of the reality we desire.

If then you do not make yourself equal to God, you cannot apprehend God; for like is known by like.
– **Hermes Trismegistus**

As the earth dances along on her journey through the cosmos, so her travels take her into regions where her energetic environment alters and this in turn has an impact upon everything and everyone who lives upon her. Just as the vibrations of one molecule can disturb the vibrations of another, so too can the subtle vibrations emanating from other celestial objects interact with those of our planetary home. When we go on a long journey in our car with the radio turned on there are times we might be listening happily to our favorite station but then we move into an area where our program is interrupted by a lot of static. We might need to shift the dial slightly so as to get clear reception. Sometimes we need to leap to a different frequency altogether. There may be times when it becomes impossible to listen to the program that we were originally tuned into, and the only alternative is to make another choice and change stations altogether.

If you are finding there's a lot of static in your life right now, and the things you were doing before aren't coming as easily as they did previously, don't yell in frustration at the radio. All you need to do is turn the dial. Tweak what you're doing slightly, or find a different station to sing along to. You may find that the new channel is much more varied, interesting and enriching.

Through a variety of innovative experiments it has been shown that our cells are primarily driven by signals from the environment or field which surrounds them. The relatively young scientific field of epigenetics has demonstrated that our genes do not control our biology but instead they act as more of a blueprint, not unlike the plan an architect would use to inform the construction of a house. A plan that can be altered by the architect if necessary. Each of our cells have structures which are remarkably like the principal organs in the human body and behave in much the same way as any intelligent human being who is capable of learning. What instigates their responses? How do these cells communicate with one another? How do they coordinate their activity? What defines their role?

Experience

Extend your arm out in front of you and wiggle your fingers. Open and close your hand. Now, move your head up and down, then from side to side. How did you just do that? Leaving aside the action of muscles, tendons, ligaments, chemicals etc., what is it that enabled that activity to take place? How did you convey your desire to the relevant component body parts? What happened in the empty space to propel your cells forward to the right location? Was there a person or some weird external force that decided to move your body in that way or was the movement made possible by your own desire? Did you have to think about it long and hard beforehand, or was the movement innate?

Become aware of the energy vibrating throughout your body

There is an old adage that, "Where attention goes, energy flows." It is the mental equivalent of tuning to a specific channel. Focus all your attention on your index finger. What do you feel? Can you feel the life force energy circulating in your finger? It is often felt as a subtle energy. It is not likely to come and hit you over the head with a great lump of wood to announce its presence, and you will probably not feel like superman/woman. It is usually, although not always, a discrete sensation. Different people feel vital energy in different ways. You may feel it as a pulsing, a tingle, a prickle or a warmth, or you may notice the blood circulating throughout your finger. Some people will sense it shooting out of the tips of their fingers. For other people it may feel cool, or like a current of air. Others might feel it more as a weight, a change of pressure or a magnetic feeling. There is no single way, no one way that is more right than another. It is a very personal experience and one which is constantly evolving. Grow accustomed to how life force energy feels as it moves throughout *your* body.

Now bring your attention to the palms of your hands. Can you feel the energy moving there? Try focusing your attention on a different part of your body – the soles of your feet, your stomach, your chest, the middle of your forehead. What do you notice? This is not something new. This vital life force energy has been circulating in your body since before the moment of your birth. It is not a hot-off-the-press phenomenon; it is as natural as breathing, but most people never take the time to notice.

Follow your breath as it flows around your body. Breath can move energy in powerful ways and amplify or calm it. Don't try to force or control the energy or your breath as it circulates throughout your body, just allow it to be present and notice the sensations. Does it feel more active in some areas and more sluggish in others? Does it feel buzzy or dense? Does it feel pleasant or uncomfortable? How do you feel right now? Don't judge, just witness. Be the observer.

Explore the energy between your hands
Place your hands so that your palms are facing each other but not quite touching. How does the air between them feel? You might find it feels warmer or denser, you may sense a change in the air pressure, or you may feel a slight tingle. Move your hands slightly further apart and feel the energy expand between them as if you

are growing an imaginary ball. Gradually increase the distance between your hands, maintaining contact with the energy as you do so.

Now hold one hand out, palm upwards. With the middle finger of your other hand trace a pattern on the palm of your hand, without making any physical contact. Can you sense the energy from your finger moving across the palm of your hand? What you are feeling is the electromagnetic fields of your hand and finger brushing one against the other.

In yoga, Indian medicine and martial arts the Sanskrit word *prana* is used to describe the subtle energy that permeates each individual and which underlies the entire cosmos. This cosmic energy comes from three principal sources: the sun, the air and the earth, as well as from secondary sources such as food, plants and water.

Notice the energy in the air

Go outside or move to an open window and fix your eyes upon one point in the sky. It is easiest if you choose a part of the sky that is neither too bright nor too shady. Continue gazing with both eyes in a relaxed and effortless way at the same spot, looking 'through' the sky rather than looking at it directly. You are looking with what is often referred to as the 'third eye', rather than your physical eyes.

To begin with you will probably start to see the 'floaters' on your eyeball: all those little particles of dust and dirt that you have tuned out so that they normally go unnoticed. You will start to become aware of little specks of sparkling white or radiant blue light, not unlike viewing amoebae under a microscope but much brighter. These are particles of prana. You will notice that they appear and disappear randomly in the sky, winking in and out of existence.

If you repeat this exercise in different locations and under different weather conditions you will realize that the amount and vibrancy of the prana changes. On sunny days and in places such as a mountaintop or the coast you will notice that there is more prana in the sky and it moves more rapidly. On an overcast day or in a city or polluted area it can be harder to see and there is less prana. It moves more sluggishly.

If you continue to stare vaguely at the sky, you may notice that the sky starts to take on a different colored tinge, or a rose pink hue. As you gaze through the sky you may also become aware of a flow of energy or of radiating patterns, like endless interconnected cobwebs wherever you place your attention.

This is the ambient life energy that is also known as *chi* or *qi* (pronounced 'chee') used by martial artists and in energy work. When a karate master effortlessly breaks a stack of bricks he is exercising his ability to cultivate, direct and transmit qi. Through qi cultivation it is possible to increase the amount of life force energy available for use, enabling us to become stronger, healthier and more vibrant.

Connect with your True self

If you want to know big mind, you must first become free of small mind.
– **Ikkyu**

Take some time each day to be still and silent. Allow yourself a few minutes to sit quietly, letting go of all external worries. When our mind is calm and peaceful it is much easier to connect with that authentic part of our self; our true self. Our brain waves shift to a lower frequency which promotes healing, increases happiness and creativity. This brings us clarity, insight and perspective. Regularly allowing the mind to be still enables us to experience an absence of fear and an inner stability that is not shaken by any outer experience.

Sit comfortably with your eyes closed and let your body relax and soften, releasing any tension. Let go of any expectations. Breathe naturally, noticing your breath as it moves in and out of your body, not changing it in any way. You may wish to use a mantra such as 'breathing in, breathing out' with each breath. Notice how you become calmer as your breath lengthens, becoming stable and rhythmic.

At first you may be surprised at how noisy and uncontrolled your mind is. Accept whatever thoughts or emotions arise. It is normal to experience interference such as mind chatter or 'monkey mind', doubt (thoughts such as 'this is ridiculous, this will never work'), aversion (emotions such as resistance, fear, anger) and restlessness. Bring all your attention to whatever arises and experience it fully, noticing any sensations you feel in your body, neither pushing them away nor following them. Gently bring your attention back to your breath.

The innate intelligence of the body is nothing short of astonishing, and modern science is still unable to explain many of its activities by any biological or neurological means.

... orthodox religion has temporarily separated the two great concepts of spirit and matter in their thought and teaching, thereby

pushing apart religion and science. The task of the new age workers is to bring these two apparent opposites together, to demonstrate that spirit and matter are not antagonistic to each other and that throughout the universe there is only spiritual substance, working on and producing the outer tangible forms.
– **Alice Bailey**

An increasing body of research supports the idea that we really are energetic beings, linked together via an underlying dynamic field. This field is both influenced by, and influences, our thoughts and emotions, our conscious and unconscious behavior and our very biology. Our physics, chemistry and biology are far from complete. Scientists have yet to find a way to deal with a conscious energy that is entirely capable of affecting the physical objects that they are studying. Our system of education and the research that stems from it is still fragmented and compartmentalized. A geneticist who is also well-versed in acoustics, electrical engineering, cosmology and musical theory remains a rare bird indeed. It is time for that to change. It's like trying to write an essay only using vowels.

What if we shifted our primary focus from that which is measurable, to a closer study of the unseen ninety-nine percent that is by and large ignored? What if we sought, instead, to better understand the links between mind and matter? What new discoveries might become available to us?

The Tao that can be told is not the eternal Tao;
The name that can be named is not the eternal name.
The nameless is the beginning of heaven and earth.
The named is the mother of ten thousand things.
Ever desireless, one can see the mystery.
Ever desiring, one can see the manifestations.
These two spring from the same source but differ in name;
This appears as darkness.

Darkness within darkness.
The gate to all mystery.
– Lao Tzu
Verse 1, *Tao Te Ching*
– As translated by **Gia-Fu Feng** *and* **Jane English**

Chapter 2

The Breath of Life

And the Lord God formed man from the dust of the ground, and breathed into his nostrils the breath of life, and man became a living soul.
– Genesis 2.7

Ruach. Pneuma. Atma. Prana. Spiritus. These are all *words* that are used to describe both breath *and* spirit in esoteric traditions across the globe, underlining that their essence is the same. A short journey through the annals of time gives us a better understanding of what the breath is all about. There are nuggets of truth to be found if we delve a little deeper into the etymology. We touch the Words in their purest form, lying buried like hidden treasure beneath the layers of dogma.

The English word 'spirit' comes from the Latin word *'spiritus'* which means 'breath, spirit, soul, courage, vigor'. It is intimately related to the word 'inspiration', derived from the Old French word *'inspiracion'*, meaning 'breathing in', 'inhaling', 'immediate influence of God or a god', 'the communication of divine instructions to the mind' and 'to impart reason to the human soul'.

The words *'breathing into'* give a sense of bringing something to life, infusing it with something, invigorating it, or influencing it in some way. From this we can see that the breath is the animating principle of all life, from which we draw our inspiration.

Prana and mind arise from the same source.
– Sri Ramana Maharshi

For yogis the breath is the external manifestation of our prana, or vital life force energy. To meditate upon the breath is to meditate upon spirit, upon consciousness, and so to become aware of awareness itself.

The notion of the breath describes the rhythmical in and out motion of life seen at all scales of existence. It denotes the benevolent inhalation of that which is fresh, new and life-enhancing, of that which nurtures and sustains us, and the releasing of that which no longer supports us for transformation.

Alchemists have long recognized spirit as a *'volatile'* substance, a distillate (the essence or concentration of something), capable of uniting fixed and unstable elements and of rendering something pure. When something is volatile it is subject to change, often suddenly and without warning. It is fleeting, transitory, unpredictable, mutable, charged, sometimes eruptive, unsettled, shifting, protean and evaporative. The word *'protean'* gives us an indication as to some of the qualities of this spirit. Named after the Greek sea god Proteus, who was renowned for his shape-shifting abilities, it is described in various dictionaries as something 'versatile, capable of doing many things, multifaceted, resourceful, multi-talented, and kaleidoscopic'. Evaporation is the process by which things change from liquid or solid states into gas or vapor due to increases in pressure and/or temperature. So it would seem that this intangible Universal substance can instigate changes in heat and pressure and has the ability to prompt significant transformation in dense physical matter, to the point that it is no longer apparent. Even the word 'apparent' offers us some insight, as it stems from an old French word meaning 'come to light'.

It is impossible to disassociate the breath from our thoughts and our emotions, or from our physical bodies. Our breath changes noticeably when we are running or sleeping, when we are exhilarated or anxious. Have you ever 'waited with bated breath' or watched someone hyperventilating when they are furious?

When we breathe, we take in air. Air, of course, contains oxygen and nitrogen, the most abundant elements in the human body, essential for our growth and nourishment, and for informing our hereditary makeup. The word used to describe air in motion is 'wind'. In the 14th century, the phrase 'long-winded' did not refer to someone who was waffling on as it does today, but to 'easy or regular breathing'. This provides clarity as to the ideal way in which to breathe. Deep, slow breathing calms the activity of the sympathetic nervous system which drives our 'fight or flight' responses and causes blood vessels to relax and widen. It lowers feelings of stress and increases blood flow to the tissues in the body and towards the heart. It stimulates the vagus nerve, so critical for optimal health, which in turn impacts upon our immune system and nearly every major organ in our body. It speeds up reaction times. It helps us to focus. It feels good.

Practitioners of Traditional Chinese Medicine and Ayurveda have recognized for centuries that the prevailing weather conditions affect our health and emotional well-being in very specific ways. They are careful to adapt their practices and to give nutritional advice which takes the seasons and climate into account. Biometeorologists study the very air that we breathe and the interactions between the biosphere and the earth's atmosphere. They examine the relationship between living organisms and conditions such as temperature, humidity and levels of light.

Throughout ancient Islam, Medieval Europe, China, India and the Americas scholars were accomplished in the art of geodesy. They recognized that an understanding of the earth's geometric shape, gravity field, orientation in space, and relationship with other planetary bodies, and how these things change over time was fundamental to their study of the tides, the magnetic poles, seismic activity, navigation, weather patterns, art, human health and much more. They understood the ways in which different angles or 'aspects' between points of interest at all scales could influence the interactions between objects, inspiring fusion, tension, friction, harmony and excitation. Traditional practices such as water-divining and Feng Shui, which translates as 'wind and water', or 'that which cannot be seen and cannot be grasped', have evolved from this geomantic knowledge. We still have much to learn.

Heaven sends down its good or evil symbols and wise men act accordingly.
– **Confucius**

Do you know someone whose joints ache when a storm is coming or a diabetic who struggles to manage their blood sugar levels during a cold front? Can you feel a headache coming on prior to a storm? Are you sensitive to solar flares and geomagnetic storms? Do you feel invigorated and cheerful on a warm sunny day?

Being able to breathe easily is vital to good health. Have you ever driven a car with a carburetor problem? The carburetor helps to meter and deliver the air-fuel mix that the engine needs to run properly. The first symptom of a failing carburetor is reduced engine performance, a reduction in power and fuel efficiency, and sluggish acceleration. Your car may backfire, spewing black smoke from the exhaust, not only burning unnecessary fuel but also producing excessive emissions and toxins. You may have difficulty starting it in cold weather and it might judder once you finally get on the road. Mountain driving can send engine temperatures rocketing, and the thinner, less compressed air can cause cars to struggle, particularly while driving through long tunnels. This is because in a given volume of air there are less molecules present as altitude increases. A buildup of residue and gummy fuel in the carburetor can cause engine failure. Sound familiar? Our bodies respond no differently. I have vivid memories of a war veteran hobbling in for a Reiki session, still soldiering on years later with numerous types of life-threatening circulation problems affecting his entire body. Prolonged periods of intense fear and unimaginable horror had taken their toll, and at some point the grief had become intolerable, too painful to deal with, so his energy system had simply contracted and all but shut down. As vital energy began to course through his body once more he lay juddering on my Reiki table just like an old car that was struggling to start on a chilly morning.

Life force energy is like a river. It needs to flow, clear and unimpeded, in order to remain healthy. We all bump into things during the course of our lives that act in much the same way as a branch falling across our own personal stream of life. Whether it is death, divorce, financial difficulty, work, family or health issues – at some point we will stumble into something that challenges us. Often, it is not the life event itself that creates a barrier across our stream, but the way in which we respond to it. If water cannot flow sometimes it will find another course, spurting out in other directions and running into areas where it might cause bother. More frequently, over time, leaves and all manner of objects that would ordinarily float on by unnoticed back up behind the original branch and start to accumulate, little by little. Eventually the stream silts up and the flow reduces to a trickle until it ceases to run altogether, becoming a gloopy, stinking, stagnant breeding ground for disease.

Air intake can affect the quality of our thoughts. Even the word 'Thy', as in 'Thy will be done', hints at this spiritual essence, at the air we breathe. It stems from the old English word 'þin'. 'Þynnian' means 'to become thin, lessen, dilute, not dense, fluid, tenuous, stretched out'. Perhaps this is why it is so easy to feel inspired and uplifted when we are in the mountains, where the air is rarefied, and our connection with nature and the elements is tangible.

At altitude the decreasing pressure causes the air particles to spread further apart. Rarefaction, the opposite of compression, decreases the density of something. Rarefaction waves expand with time. Conversely when pressure is increased the opposite happens. Rarefaction occurs naturally in the layers of the earth's atmosphere due to the gravitation of the planet. Compression and rarefaction are characteristic of the propagating pressure wave we more commonly refer to as sound. The humble tuning fork, an acoustic resonator used for tuning musical instruments, as the time-keeping element in clocks and watches, and in vibrational healing therapies, creates repeating longitudinal patterns of compression and rarefaction as it vibrates. The relevance of this should become clear later in this book. Given the high quantity of water molecules in the human body it is worthy of note at this point that moisture rarefies when heated.

In cultures all around the world, the peaks of sacred mountains are places of myth and legend, where we are closest to the Divine. We are literally elevated above the mundane and ordinary. We slip naturally into a feeling of awe at the magnificence that surrounds us, and can more readily release the turbulent strife of our stressful lives.

Climb the mountains and get their good tidings.
Nature's peace will flow into you as sunshine flows into trees.
The winds will blow their own freshness into you,
And the storms their own energy,
While cares will drop off like autumn leaves.
– **John Muir**

At extreme altitudes hallucinations, visions and distortions of bodily senses are a well-known phenomenon amongst intrepid mountain explorers. One world-class mountaineer recalls hearing someone speaking French while alone at altitude on a mountaintop:

The voice seemed to emanate from within my own body, and I heard myself responding. It was in French too – amazing, if you consider that I don't speak French at all.

Another climber tells of meeting a mysterious man some 8200 meters up the southeast ridge of Mount Everest, well into the infamous 'death zone'. The stranger climbed with him for 10 hours, chatting along the way and encouraging him to keep moving and to change his oxygen cylinder, before inexplicably vanishing near the climb's end.

These our actors, as I foretold you, were all Spirits, and are melted into Ayre, into thin Ayre.
– **Shakespeare, *The Tempest***

The word 'wind' tells us about the motion of the air itself. It moves by 'twisting, turning, curling, swinging, plaiting and weaving' according to the Old English word *'windan'*. How often have you 'turned things over' in your mind? When someone's thoughts are distorted or confused we often say they have a 'twisted mind'. This twisting, weaving movement is described to perfection by the Torus vortex, a dynamic process that can be found in sustainable systems at all scales. It allows for a smoothly continuous and uniform energy exchange and flow of information throughout the whole of creation. We see it in the water that corkscrews down a plughole or drain, in the bubble rings blown by whales and dolphins, in the twisting air of the tornado and as a frequency converter in electrical engineering. It can be found in the magnetic fields around atoms, people, planets and entire galaxies.

Consisting of a central axis with a vortex at either end, energy flows into the first vortex, through the center, and out via the other vortex, wrapping around itself to return to its starting point. We find it symbolized in the Taoist yin and yang symbol, and in the tail-chasing dragon. Energy in perpetual motion constantly whirls back to itself in a continuous loop, ever contracting and expanding like the breath itself, twisting and turning as it does so. At its center is a point of absolute stillness and balance at which all forces are equal. This still point, which Buckminster Fuller described as the vector equilibrium, is considered by many to be the primary structure upon which sacred geometry is founded, a cornerstone for the building blocks of life.

Masters of Aikido, the art of the peaceful warrior, have an intimate understanding of this pattern of energy flow. Using a minimum of effort, they endeavor to move in harmony with the path of this whirling, powerful flow of 'ki', ultimately becoming one with their opponent and with life force energy itself.

Aiki is not a technique to fight with or defeat an enemy. It is the way to reconcile the world and make human beings one family.
– Morihei Ueshiba

The word weaving offers a sense of combining something into a whole. The *'Indra's Net'* of the Buddhist faith begins to make more sense. Something is woven using a regular, systematic and orderly method or pattern of weaving. It is an ongoing, continuing process.

The journey, not the destination matters.
– TS Eliot

For me these words immediately bring to mind the constantly flowing, interlacing, interlocking patterns I see moving in waves throughout the sky like endless cobwebs. Often, when I gaze into the sky or stare into 'empty' space, I find myself wondering if I am watching thoughts in motion and whether snowflakes simply provide a snapshot of a moment in consciousness, temporarily frozen in time and space by the prevailing weather conditions. A whole sky full of Masaru Emoto-like water crystals. I have come to realize that space is not empty at all, but teeming with activity that was previously invisible to me.

The whole universe appears as a dynamic web of inseparable energy patterns... Thus we are not separated parts of a whole. We are a whole.
– **Barbara Brennan**

The past tense of weave was once *'wave'*, rather than *'wove'* as it is today. In astrological symbolism, the wavelike glyph for the air sign Aquarius, the water bearer, pertains to air waves. Aquarius is ruled by both Saturn and Uranus, a planet which is particularly associated with attributes such as the higher mind, electricity, intuition, vision, innovation, imagination, originality, progressive thinking, unpredictability, humanitarianism and enlightenment. In Ancient Greek mythology, Uranus was known as Father Sky, the son and husband of Gaia, Mother Earth, who he would cover every night. Some cite Aether, one of the primordial deities, as a personification of the upper air breathed by the gods, as opposed to the air breathed by mortals.

We tend to think of air as relatively uniform, because the tiny changes that are continually taking place all around us are imperceptible, but in reality air is in constant movement. Just as every raindrop that falls upon a pond creates expanding concentric circles which continue unimpeded, even when the circles interact with the patterns made by another droplet, so too does every word we utter, every thought we think, have an impact in the air.

When we speak we move air. Our breath becomes audible. Today the word 'conspire' has a completely different connotation to the one it once held. Originally it meant 'to unite, to agree', 'breathing with' or 'sounding together'. Little wonder that indigenous communities are said to be able to affect the weather with their joint prayer and sacred rituals.

When we 'get wind of something' we receive information about it. When we say we are 'winded' we mean that we are tired, out of breath or have been rendered temporarily breathless.

Being winded is often used to refer to that feeling when we have been punched in the abdomen or solar plexus and the air is knocked out of us. The Japanese refer to this important area as the Hara and see it as an ocean or reservoir of energy, the seat of life. It is not by chance that the umbilical cord is situated in this part of the body. It is the oxygen-rich center of the etheric or chi body and provides a gateway to the planet's etheric field which lies beyond time and space. It interacts with all of the body's organs, especially the intestines, fueling and nurturing the body-mind in a variety of ways, and is seen as a center of power and vitality. Hara is a hub of vibrational activity. A blow to this area produces a compression of the complex network of nerves situated there, which causes the diaphragm to go into spasm. This makes breathing difficult and painful, frequently inducing anxiety and panic. Slow deep inhalation into the stomach relieves the problem.

The word 'Hara' is used to describe the quality of a person's energy. One may be said to have 'good' or 'bad' Hara. Hara diagnosis plays a crucial role in Eastern medicine. All movements in Japanese martial arts originate in the Hara, our center of gravity, both physically and spiritually. When someone anchors themselves in the Hara they become composed and balanced, shaking off external disturbances and returning to their power of 'original being'. In this way their work is accomplished easily and without effort.

The Hara... the source of vital Chi... is the gate of breathing.
– The Nan Ching

When you have a disease, do not try to cure it. Find your center and you will be healed. There are some things that can be sensed but not explained in words.
– Taoist proverb

Experience - Breathing into the Hara

When you are feeling disempowered, lacking in confidence, or struggling to find answers, place your attention onto your Hara, a couple of centimeters below the tummy button, and mentally bring your breath there. Allow your posture to become more open and expansive. Notice how it makes you feel and how much more easily you respond to the situation you are facing. When our awareness is in our Hara we can respond with our whole being, not just with our mind and emotions.

Man, as a living being, is not rooted in himself. Rather is he nourished, sustained and held in order by Nature whose laws operate without his knowledge and assistance. Man sets himself in opposition to the order of life which fundamentally sustains him if, by an unnatural shifting of his center of gravity, he denies that vital center in his bearing which testifies to this order.

– Karlfried Graf Dürckheim

The longest-lived animals on this planet also happen to be those that have the slowest rate of breathing. The average human at rest takes between 12–16 breaths per minute, while a practiced yogi will breathe between 4–10 breaths per minute. Slow, conscious breathing can help us to live longer, healthier lives.

This breath of life affects not only our bodies, but the earth itself. A knowledge of the structural response of minerals to changes in temperature and pressure is of primary importance to the earth sciences. In crystallography, for example, air, heat, pressure and magnetics directly influence the ordered arrangements of atoms, ions and molecules, and the symmetric repeating patterns within crystalline structures.

The role of the Chinese Geomancer is to determine the flow of the magnetic 'lung-mei', dragon currents or dragon's breath, that undulate across our planet, understanding how they are influenced by the position of the sun, moon and the five major planets. Every structure, every tree, is placed within the landscape in accordance with a precise geometric system using laws of math and music in such a way as to work in harmony with the forces of nature. While the relevance of the word lung to the breath is obvious, the word *'mei'* is less apparent but equally important. In Chinese and Japanese it can mean to sprout or dance, bright, alliance, ring and echo.

The name *'Mei'* is closely related to the names *'Maya'* and *'Mae'*. In both Hinduism and Buddhism Maya is 'the supernatural power by which the universe becomes manifest; the illusion or appearance of the phenomenal world'. In Nepalese Maya means 'love'. Derived from the Sanskrit word *'mā'*, to create, it is the root of words such as 'material', 'matter' and 'measure'. Mae can be found as an affix in words such as maestro, Maecenas and maenad, all of which allude to someone with the ability to impart rich, inspired counsel for the growth, enlightenment and upliftment of humanity.

The Incas call such currents *'spirit lines'*, while aboriginals refer to them as *'song lines'* or *'dreaming tracks'*. They have also been known as *Wouivre* and *Wyvern*, stemming from the old French word for snake, *'guivre'*, a mythical creature similar to a dragon, and the Latin word *'vipera'* meaning 'viper'. Viper is itself a contraction of the words *'vivipera'*, from the Latin word *'vivus'* meaning 'alive' and 'living' and the word *'parire'* meaning 'bringing forth' and 'bear'. The Oracle of Delphi, High Priestess of the Temple of Apollo, was known as Pythia, the serpent woman. She prophesied from within a cave in the depths of the earth and was said to take her powers from a female dragon dwelling in the Castalian Spring where the sacred waters were the source of her inspired elucidations. There at the Omphalos Stone, then considered to be the 'navel of the world' from which terrestrial life originated, she would breathe in the vapors from a chasm in the earth and fall into a trance through which she could access Divine wisdom.

... neither her face nor hue went untransformed; Her breast heaved; Her heart grew large with passion. Taller to their eyes, sounding no longer mortal, she prophesied what was inspired from The God breathing near, uttering words not to be ignored.
– **Virgil,** *Aeneid*

The renowned philosopher and scientist Aristotle's first wife was called Pythias the Elder. She herself was an accomplished biologist and embryologist. Could she also have been a valuable source of wisdom and inspiration for her husband?

In cultures around the world serpents represent creative life force, and are guardians of treasure and of sacred sites. Even the name of the great sage and philosopher Pythagoras alludes to this powerful, weaving kundalini energy that allows access to an expanded state of consciousness. Kundalini is a Sanskrit term describing the primal energy which lies curled at the base of the spine until it is awakened. Also referred to as Shakti or the sleeping goddess, once enlivened this extremely powerful spiritual energy will seek to rise to meet her male counterpart Shiva in the crown, and in so doing bring gifts of inner wisdom. This coming together of masculine and feminine principles represents the union of human and divine consciousness, the awakened mind. If we do not bring awareness to our actions we behave in a way that is disordered and ignorant. Conversely, dormant awareness requires energy if it is to create.

I am trying to awake the energy contained in the air. These are the main sources of energy. What is considered as empty space is just a manifestation of matter that is not awakened.
– **Nikola Tesla**

The links between the breath, spiritual energy with its life-giving properties and Divine revelation are clear. This life force energy that flows to us and through us is not something that we are separate from. It is a natural human potential.

There shall no strange god be in thee; neither shalt thou worship any strange god.
– **Psalms 81.9**

Simple breath meditation

Most people are unaware of their breath unless they are having difficulty breathing, and much less able to perceive the part of the breath that gives life to the mind.

Sit comfortably with your hands upon your knees or thighs, palms facing either upwards or downwards, or with one placed lightly on top of the other. Keep your mouth gently closed, with your tongue resting just behind slightly parted teeth and a relaxed jaw. This simple position connects the front and back energy channels, the two polar axes, and helps to balance yin and yang throughout the body. Sitting upright encourages the upward movement of life force energy. Shift your gaze downwards and close your eyes. This will prevent visual distractions and reduce brain-wave activity by as much as 75 percent. Breathe in and out easily through your nose. This helps to calm the mind. Quietly bring all your attention to the area just in front of your face at the tip of your nose. Keep focused upon this point, where the true breath is experienced. It is a meeting place between physical and nonphysical. Do not force your breath into any particular rhythm or pattern, just allow it to be exactly as it is. Notice the sensations that you feel here. To begin with your attention will most likely be upon your physical breath but as you retain your focus the sensations will become increasingly refined, allowing you to become aware of the much subtler movements that animate life.

Notice the in-breath and the out-breath, and realize that they are in fact one process. Each inhalation and exhalation are simply manifestations of the two poles that exist in all things. The breath may be silent, or may make a particular noise. You may become aware of your inner sounds. When energy moves it causes a vibration which produces many discrete noises with different frequencies, harmonies and rhythms. Notice the breath itself, not the path of the breath. Don't follow the breath into the body, just remain as a detached observer. You may notice a magnetic push-pull sensation, or a switching of polarities. When awareness is drawn into the body then positive, yang energy is predominant. When we place this awareness outside the body then negatively charged yin energy predominates. When we keep our attention on the 'nose-tip' then the two come into perfect balance, into a place of non-duality, a meeting point of the experience and that which is experienced.

You may experience the breath as a presence rather than a movement or become aware of various sensory impressions, physical, emotional or mental. This is perfectly normal. Allow whatever sensations that arise to be present without judging them, but remain focused upon this one point.

Try placing your attention on this area while you are out walking, reading or going about things in your normal daily life. You will find it will help you to remain present and will bring you clarity, focus and insight.

Alternate nostril breathing

A great way to purify the subtle energy channels is to breathe through one nostril at a time. This incredibly simple technique can calm the emotions, improve sleep, help with circulation and respiration, increase energy and improve clarity. The nostrils are directly linked to the brain and nervous system.

You may not have noticed, but we don't usually breathe equally through both nostrils at the same time. Single nostril breathing helps to balance the left and right sides of our brains. When we breathe in through our left nostril we access the right hemisphere of our brains: our feminine, feeling, creative, intuitive, emotional side. Conversely, when we breathe in through our right nostril we access the thinking side of our brain: our masculine, logical, analytical self. Make a 'peace sign' with your right hand, then tuck the two extended fingers onto the palm of your hand. Place your thumb gently on your right nostril, and your ring and little fingers onto your left. Keeping your mouth closed throughout, use your right thumb to close the right nostril and inhale slowly, deeply, and smoothly through your left nostril. Pause for a second then close your left nostril with your ring and little fingers, taking your thumb off the right nostril. Exhale through your right nostril, then inhale through your right nostril. Pause again, then use your thumb to close off the right nostril, release your fingers from your left nostril and exhale through your left nostril. Repeat this several times, without any effort. Begin with just a few repetitions and build up gradually over time.

For breath is life, and if you breathe well you will live long upon this earth.
– **Sanskrit proverb**

Chapter 3

Thoughts Are Things

As a man thinketh in his heart so is he.
– Proverbs 23.7

While thought may seem like a subtle, nebulous thing, it is an actual force, a substance that is every bit as 'real' as electricity, light, or any dense and solid object. We are permanently surrounded by a vast ocean of thought that is constantly flowing to us and through us. Thinking is a creative process of life that is in perpetual motion. It's what minds do. We can no more stop thinking than we can stop breathing.

There is no greater power in the universe than thought. Our ability to think is infinite and inexhaustible. Thought travels incredibly quickly – much faster than the speed of sound – and is not limited by time or distance. Think of someone you know who lives on the other side of the world. How long did it take you to bring them to mind? Think of something you did last week, ten years ago. Think ahead to something you anticipate doing in the future. The process is virtually instantaneous.

Our thoughts, words and actions *all* belong to the world of gross matter, not to the ethereal realm. Our thoughts may be invisible to the naked eye but they nevertheless manifest within the world of fine gross matter. Our words operate in the realm of medium gross matter, and our actions take place within the world of dense, or coarse, gross matter. Thoughts, words and actions are intimately related to one another, interwoven.

Our thoughts are no less connected to something that can be seen and felt in the material realm than a shadow with the object it replicates. In the same way that a shadow points us to the physical reality, physical reality indicates the nature of thought.

Human thinking is the shadowing forth of ideas and beings belonging to a higher world...
– **Rudolf Steiner**

This mirroring may take place within the current material reality, within the etheric world or across other timelines or lifetimes, but it will nevertheless take place. Everything you see around you right now has occurred as a result of your previous thinking.

All is mind.
– **The Kybalion**

Once it is understood that every thought is a vibrational, spiritual form in its own right, evolving, developing, molding and shaping itself continually, then much becomes clear. A thought will radiate outwards, often outliving the body in which it was initiated, yet it always remains attached to its point of origin, and will sooner or later come spiraling back. Thus, the value of mindfulness becomes apparent. Every thought-creation will one day return to us.

And their works do follow them!
– **Revelation 14.13**

As a thought arises, with varying degrees of intensity, so an ethereal form is produced. Because thoughts operate within the field of fine gross matter, they are not usually visible or audible. I use the word *'usually'* quite intentionally. On more than one occasion I have clearly heard words that I know I have just thought while playing back the recording of online healing sessions, particularly when they were amplified by emotion. Each time the word repeated itself distinctly several times, but rather than fading away like an echo, it became increasingly louder as if spiraling through a vortex. Of course, this is only my personal experience, yet to be scientifically validated, but it would seem to be an area worthy of further exploration.

If you want to know the quality of your thoughts then take a look around you. Without exception, your personal environment and your relationships will provide you with clear feedback, acting as a mirror for your former thinking.

Thought, of which we are both senders and receivers, has electromagnetic properties and thrives upon association. Both consciously and unconsciously, we collect data to support our beliefs. We readily accept ideas that fit in with our particular beliefs, and reject, or repel, others. Like thoughts inevitably attract other like thoughts. Each thought will inexorably draw others of a similar vibration towards them, or will seek to join others of a similar nature. How often have you had a thought about a person or a situation that began life as an irritating niggle, but within no time built it into something far greater in your mind? The ego loves to stew upon such thoughts for weeks, months or years on end if left unchecked. Perhaps somebody did or said something that caused offence, which in and of itself wasn't a big deal. "They did that last time," the ego might whisper, or, "They always do that," "They'll probably do it again in the future," "They did other things that hurt," "Come to think of it, that woman last week did something similar," "People are always doing hurtful things," "I always end up getting hurt," "Poor me, poor me," "I wouldn't treat someone like that," "I'm much better than them." In a matter of moments the irritation, whisked into a downward spiral of self-pitying thought, has escalated to resentment or anger. That grain of sand in your shoe is now a lump of gravel. How often do we get out of bed on the wrong side only to watch our day go downhill from there? We only have to step barefoot into cat-sick first thing in the morning or have somebody bump into our car on the drive to work to see how quickly our day disintegrates when we're not tending carefully to the quality of our thoughts.

Of course, this works the other way too. We all know a

relentlessly sunny Pollyanna, whose life always seems to be working out perfectly with consummate ease. How lucky they seem. How blessed their lives are. There is no chance at play here, nothing random. Like electricity, the creative Universe is neutral. It doesn't judge or discriminate. No one is ever told, "You're not good enough to iron that shirt," as they push the plug into a socket. "You're not worthy of watching TV tonight" or "You haven't studied enough to boil a kettle." It doesn't distinguish between 'good thoughts' and 'bad thoughts'. It simply responds to the thoughts and emotions that we feed it. Pollyanna just happens to keep feeding it more 'happy'.

> *Until you make the unconscious conscious, it will control your life and you will call it fate.*
> **– Carl Jung**

Focused attention is a key principle in all energy work. Where attention goes, energy flows. We will always get more of whatever we focus upon. Just as Facebook algorithms are designed to give us a better experience by showing us more posts of the type that we recently liked and commented on, or from the friends we last interacted with, so the Universe will generously provide us with more of whatever we engage with. Facebook doesn't know that we would prefer to see posts from certain friends. If we haven't connected with them recently, then they won't appear in our newsfeed until we start doing so.

Each thought has a frequency and translates as an inner sound or vibration, but thoughts will also strive to materialize. A thought has structure, just as an atom, a molecule, or a table leg does. One thought attracts another, which attracts another, and another, together gaining in strength, until eventually they manifest in our physical reality with some solidity. The type of thought can easily be felt in the body. Some thoughts feel light; others feel heavy and weigh us down. Just as a stone will sink to the bottom of a bowl of water and a cork will bob to the top, so the soul becomes lighter or heavier through the nature of repeated patterns of thinking. The rules of density and gravity apply as equally in the nonmaterial world as they do in the world we see around us.

If we don't like what we are seeing around us then we simply have to change our thoughts. We can *always* change our thoughts, and thus it is always possible to create a different situation from every now moment. Indeed, if we keep on thinking the same thoughts about a situation it is highly unlikely that it will change without assistance from some outside force.

It matters not if we are focused upon something that we don't want in our lives. Equally, placing our attention upon the absence of something will produce more of the absence of it. This infinite Universe of ours will always find us something that matches whatever we are concentrating on.

Notice what you are thinking and feeling
Set an alarm or mindfulness app so that every hour or every half an hour you get an alert. Stop whatever you are doing for a few seconds and pay attention to what you are currently thinking or feeling. Ask yourself, "What am I thinking right now?" If you are mentally or emotionally engaged with something that supports you, great, give yourself a mental cheer. If not, don't beat yourself up, but simply turn your attention to something that feels better.
The next time an event, wanted or unwanted, occurs in your life ask yourself what thoughts you had been preoccupied with immediately prior.
It is only when we become aware of our habitual thought patterns and emotional responses that we can start to change them. To begin with, you may be horrified to learn what occupies your mind for the

greatest portion of the day. Don't worry. Although habitual patterns of thinking may have taken a lifetime to learn, you will soon start to recognize unhelpful thought patterns and their links to events that happen in your life. Ask yourself questions such as, "Is this true?" or "What is the underlying fear?" Notice how you feel in your body as you think the thought. Where do you feel tension, discomfort, contraction? Little by little, you will find yourself with uplifting thoughts in your head when the timer goes off, and you will begin to celebrate the good things in life that occur as a result. The first step is to become aware of your habitual thinking.

Thankfully, there are two sides to everything in this world of duality, and once we begin to become consciously aware of our thoughts we can always choose others. Within each active thought its polar opposite lies in a passive state. From thoughts of disease we can create thoughts of well-being. We can shift from thinking about poverty to thinking of plenty, or from feeling stuck to thinking about the many ways in which we feel movement and express ourselves freely. Once we start to do so we will naturally attract more thoughts of a like kind, and it is these new thoughts that will gain momentum. Cultivate your mind as you would tend a garden. Nature doesn't distinguish between the seeds we plant; therefore, sow only the types of seeds you wish to grow. You will never watch poppies come into bloom if you've sown a garden full of thistles. The same amount of energy goes into growing a weed as it does to growing a flower. As long as we allow things to seem real to us we are giving them our energy, nurturing them and keeping them alive. Pull out weeds by their roots before they have had time to gain strength. Rather than allowing new weeds to take their place, fill the bare soil that is left behind with beautiful, scented new plants that lift your spirit. Make your garden a wonderful place in which to dwell.

*Keep the hearth of your thoughts pure, by so doing you will bring
peace and be happy!*
– Abd-Ru-Shin

True mindfulness requires discipline and regular practice but it is
well worth the effort.

*As a single footstep will not make a path on the earth, so a single
thought will not make a pathway in the mind. To make a deep
physical path, we walk again and again. To make a deep mental
path, we must think over and over the kind of thoughts we wish to
dominate our lives.*
– Henry David Thoreau

Mindfulness literally rewires the brain, creating new neural
pathways and new ways of responding to the triggers of life. Such
awareness does not mean we deny certain thoughts, afraid or
ashamed of what might have crossed our minds. Resistance and
still more resistance just generate friction. We can no more repress
thought than we can restrain lightning, but it doesn't mean we
have to stand outside in the middle of a storm. We don't deny
torrential rain; we accept its presence, knowing it is beyond our
control and that sunny days will follow.

Don't be surprised,
Don't be startled;
All things will arrange themselves.
Don't cause a disturbance,
Don't exert pressure;
All things will clarify themselves.
– Huainanzi

Often the easiest way to counter 'stinking thinking' is simply to put our attention elsewhere, upon something better-feeling. Meditate, go for a nap, do some art, dance, paint – anything in which we are in a state of non-resistance that doesn't nourish the unwanted still further.

Generally speaking, imagination and emotion follow thought. Imagination is an extremely powerful tool of manifestation. It is irrelevant that there is not yet any tangible evidence of that which is desired in the current physical reality. All that exists within this time-space reality is based upon intangible, untouchable thought, the energetic blueprint of structural reality. Imagining how things might be is like picking up a pencil and starting to sketch the floor plan of a house. Just because the finance for the build and the construction team have not yet materialized, and no bricks have yet been laid, it does not mean that the build is not soon going to get underway. There are endless options for construction, decoration, and other home comforts. Once something has been imagined then the potential for it exists, even though there may be a delay during which the project comes to maturity and the component parts come together. There are unlimited, infinite possibilities in the Universe. Our imagination sets their vibrational version into motion.

Emotions amplify and propel thought. Imagination and emotion are the most concentrated forms of energy available to us as human beings. Indeed, studies have shown that participants have had physically measurable results simply by imagining and 'feeling' that they are exercising, without actually undertaking any exercise. Bodies respond to imagination and emotion, regardless of the physical reality. Flexibility and range of movement can also be demonstrably and significantly improved through thought alone.

Of course, the type of thought we are talking about here is not of the fleeting, unruly kind, but that which involves our sustained, focused attention. It's not necessary that we dedicate hours and hours to such contemplation. Indeed, only a very short period of the sort of imaginative thinking that engages our emotions, in such a way that we generate the same feelings that we might experience if we were actually physically doing what we were thinking about, can be enough to inspire a physical transformation. Only a short period of pure thought, i.e. a simple thought without another thought contradicting it, will attract another of the same tone and vibration. Shortly afterwards the two thoughts will join, creating an expanded energy, a point of combustion. This generates a feeling of enthusiasm or interest that bubbles within us, and the original thought becomes bigger, more evolved, and vibrates more rapidly. If we can repeat this process we generate a thought of a higher, faster vibration. Soon we will have generated enough combustion to influence physical manifestation. Only a few hours of concentrated thought are equivalent to many, many hours of action.

If we are in a good-feeling place while focused upon that which we wish to see materialize, if we are in alignment with that greater part of ourselves, then things fall into place with astonishingly little effort on our part. Just being in that good-feeling place while we are getting on with living our lives is a blessing in and of itself.

In reality, we often vacillate between two points of focus. From an early age we have been taught to weigh up the pros and cons of a situation. This is all part of the maturing process of thought, and provides us with the contrast necessary to make choices that please us. Once a decision has been reached, it is imperative to ensure that attention remains focused on that which has been decided upon; otherwise, the energy of the thought that was generated becomes divided. This split energy can be draining, and 'scattered thinking' is at the root of much physical illness. If we are waiting for a heavy pot to boil over an open fire, we don't keep taking it on and off the heat. We would wear ourselves out, and the pot would take much longer to boil.

Instead, we simply leave it to bubble away rapidly and allow the necessary heat and pressure changes to take place, until the water reaches the temperature required.

We may start to think one thing, and then contrast it with an opposing thought. We begin to form a thought and then quickly contradict ourselves partway through. We form thoughts such as, "I really want to live in a peaceful home, I so wish my kids would stop fighting," "I am determined to feel well, I am sick to death of being ill," or "I want more money, I'm tired of being broke." This is equivalent to a mental tug-of-war, and the dominant thought is the one that will prevail. If there is no opposing thought *active* on the other end of the rope, the rope will move with very little resistance to your chosen spot.

A great many people make a life choice, and then spend long periods mulling over the 'what if' that they initially rejected. They leave a relationship, yet think incessantly about the person they chose to move on from, often becoming jealous or demonstrating other dysfunctional behavior when the person that they left forms a new partnership. They stay with someone to whom they are no longer suited, and then make themselves sick with resentment. They choose a career path that they find doesn't please them, and put all their energy into regretting the decision they made instead of finding ways they can evolve their career opportunities. This is like driving off into your new life but leaving the handbrake on.

Just as we can always form a different thought, we can always make another choice. Like an ever-expanding fractal, life is a series of decisions, of choice points through which we continually evolve.

If you don't change directions, you may end up where you are heading.
– **Lao Tzu**

Our thoughts cause our energy body to contract and expand. As we spend more time thinking uplifting thoughts, so our energy body expands and vibrates at a faster rate. Not only does this enable things to manifest into our physical reality more quickly, but it also allows us to develop a robust, healthy, energetic 'immune system'. Many people who are interested in esoteric subjects spend inordinate amounts of time considering ways in which they might protect themselves psychically and energetically from the thoughts, emotions and actions of others. Of course, in so doing, their attention is focused upon something that is entirely rooted in fear, and thus they are far more likely to create the sort of experience in which they will need to protect themselves. Their time would be far better invested in practicing purity of thought. By mentally exploring the myriad of ways they might feel happy and expansive, they will simultaneously draw others who reflect these qualities to themselves. As the quality of our thought improves, so does our personal situation.

In some cultures, particularly those in which legends of witchcraft and magick abound, there are long-standing traditions of hex-casting upon others, usually for the most mundane of reasons, such as boundary disputes or arguments over livestock. It goes without saying that this is a most unwise practice, as all thoughts invariably return to their point of origin, amplified, through the action of the Law of Returns. No thought, on its own, will do significant harm to another. Each of us accepts only those thoughts and ideas that fit in with our own system of beliefs. We are not entirely at the mercy of unconscious events.

By allowing ourselves to feel good and think happy thoughts, we effortlessly form a natural defense against psychic attack, whether it was intended or otherwise. The body's innate wisdom will always seek to come back into balance and will correct errors of perception if we allow it the opportunity to do so. Not only does our energy body expand so that such thoughts are either deflected or substantially diminished, their vibration making only the barest of ripples, but our surplus of good-feeling will spontaneously bubble over so that the abundance is shared with others.

If we are all interconnected, who or what are we protecting ourselves from? Does a wave need to protect itself from crashing into other waves, or are all waves simply part of the same body of water? On occasion, a certain vibration in the energy field of another may resonate with something that already exists in our own field, triggering an uncomfortable feeling. This offers a great opportunity for inward reflection. We can ask ourselves questions such as, "What thought or belief do I hold that makes me feel this way?" "What am I thinking that is out of alignment with my true nature?" or "How can I reframe this?" There is no requirement for bubbles of protection, or angelic shields and capes in an energetic toolbox. The energetically robust are those who are grounded and unshakeable in their knowledge that all is well. Energetic protection is a response that is based upon a belief that something is wrong, in the sort of fear-based thinking that produces contraction. On the contrary, each time we share our love, compassion and joy with others, the same thing is reflected back in a multitude of ways, and so the physical, emotional, mental and spiritual bodies are fortified still further.

Information does not exist in isolation, nor is it inert. It is connected to the consciousness of all those who understand it, or from whom it originates, and will naturally gravitate to those who seek it. In practice, our thought is seldom original but is merely a collection of teachings, habits and belief constructs already in existence which have been handed down from generation to generation.

All truly wise thoughts have been thought already thousands of times; but to make them truly ours we must think them over again honestly till they take root in our personal experience.
– **Johann von Goethe**

We have a tendency to tinker around the edges of existing ideas. The deep thinker is most uncommon, but it is from such contemplation – upon that which exists within the spiritual realms, beyond time and space – that true innovation arises. There are no problems that cannot be solved with right-thinking.

Intellect is the highest of what is earthly, and is meant to be the steering element through life on earth, whereas the driving power is the intuitive perception, which originates in the Spiritual World.
– Abd-Ru-Shin

The longer we retain a thought in our mind before speaking about it or acting upon it, the greater its power becomes.

Consciousness is active and spontaneous. It loves to play, to explore and to be inventive. While there is a clear benefit to being mindful of what we are creating with our thoughts, constant self-examination goes against the very nature of consciousness. We would be wise to pay attention to our predominant mental state, because it will determine our subsequent experiences, but there is no need to be afraid of our thoughts. They are just thoughts. They are not who we are. Left to their own devices, thoughts will just pass on by. It is only when we attach some importance to them, or judge and label them in some way that they begin to take on form.

We are neither our thoughts, nor our emotions. What we are is far grander and more spacious than that. If this makes little sense to you, ask yourself, "Who is the thinker of this thought?" Thoughts and emotions are like clouds in the sky. They are just weather. Sometimes the clouds are sparse and few and far between; sometimes they gather ominously in a dark grey mass upon the horizon. But no matter how many clouds exist the sky is always present, the sun is still shining even though we might not be able to see it, and the clouds will pass sooner or later. The clouds no more control or define the sky, than our thoughts control the witnessing presence, the essence that exists behind them. This is why meditation is such a powerful tool. When we allow ourselves to sit quietly in a state of non-attachment to our thoughts, we are closest to our natural state of being, and the subsequent nature of thought that arises is pure and uncontaminated. This is the type of keen thinking by which we would be wise to allow our lives to be directed.

Let us consider, now, our perception of our unique identity. In our physical bodies, cells are constantly dying and replenishing themselves. Yet despite all this apparent destruction and rebirth, our sense of identification with the self remains stable. Over the years we may age – largely in a way that directly correlates with our beliefs about the process of ageing – but we don't dissolve into a messy puddle each time a batch of cells rejuvenates. Our organs, our bones, our teeth, our hair, our so-called blemishes, our physical bodies in their entirety, retain their form. So, too, our sense of identity remains secure, despite the many changes it undergoes throughout a lifetime. The adult version of you may no longer believe in Santa Claus, but you are no less you than you were all those years ago.

Just as you hold conscious and subconscious memories about your sense of self, so too do each cell, each atom, each molecule in your body. The conscious self may be oblivious to them, but the True Self is always aware of its identity. Every single life experience is retained, indelibly etched into that which remains primarily below the threshold of conscious awareness. This filter is a wonderful mechanism indeed. Would you want to be aware of every single bodily process that is taking place at any moment, let alone all those processes that have happened in the past? Of course not. It would be too overwhelming. Our minds are designed to focus on other, more pertinent things. Nevertheless, these memories are etched into our very cellular structure, and our conscious thoughts have the ability to catapult past events into our vibrational awareness. Current circumstances can trigger thoughts and feelings about past events, whether they be uplifting or traumatic. These can present themselves unmistakably in the mind and in the body, or they can be discrete and subtle, for example a nagging feeling in the gut that something is 'off'.

Our conscious and unconscious thoughts direct the way the cells in the body function, even though we may not consciously be aware of how each cell is meant to operate. Every cell not only holds the data relating to its own experiences, but also has an innate awareness of what has been and is currently going on throughout the entire body and is able to respond accordingly. A change in one cell will be noted in the body consciousness, or the collective consciousness if you like, and will cause other cells to consider the potentials, to evaluate and make a prediction, and to respond accordingly. The memories and beliefs stored within each cell are constantly being transmitted, with the body making continual adjustments to adapt to the prevailing thought environment. Our perception of something will impact upon the body's response to it, changing things like brain and blood chemistry, heart rate and respiration. The body and mind will work diligently together to come into vibrational coherence, thus creating a material reality that accurately reflects the predominant mental state. We are, quite literally, our thoughts and emotions manifested as physical form.

Children spend the first few years of their formative lives primarily in a theta brain-wave state, which enables them to effortlessly and unconsciously absorb the thoughts, emotions and beliefs of those closest to them. This is nature's way of helping us to quickly learn the necessary skills to adapt and survive in any given environment. Just like someone with a brand-new computer, they download the programs and patterns of behavior that are appropriate for the task they need to do. However, a parent's prevailing belief may not always be one that is healthy and constructive for us. It is nevertheless highly likely to become assimilated until our life experience causes us to challenge its validity. A study of adopted children raised in families with a history of hereditary cancers showed that they are as likely to develop cancer as those children in the same family with totally different genetics. It is for this very reason that, if presented with a child who has become sick at a young age, most professional healers and shamans will want to liaise closely with the parents, often undertaking work that radically challenges their underlying beliefs.

Our beliefs are the lens through which we view life, operating assumptions upon which we judge ourselves, base all our decisions and take action. Our inner environments create our external world, with our thoughts and beliefs affecting not only our physical bodies but the reality that we see before us. We project our thoughts, that which we feel about ourselves, outwards onto others. Those around us thus provide direct feedback as to what we are really thinking and feeling about ourselves, often subconsciously, and offer us some big clues as to the ways in which we are out of alignment with our higher nature. If we find ourselves surrounded by people who lie, we should closely examine the ways in which we are not being honest with ourselves. If we constantly seem to be attracting life's complainers, it would be sensible to ask how often we are focused upon the downside of life rather than its positive aspects, and how often we express appreciation and gratitude for all life has to offer.

Our collectively-held thoughts also have a big impact upon our lives. If, as it is suggested here, we do indeed create our own realities with our thoughts and our point of focus, then it is clear that our current collective reality is the result of many generations of muddled, poorly focused collective thinking. For example, if there is a commonly-held belief that all politicians are corrupt, then what sort of politics do you think we are likely to see around us? In what ways do they mirror our own behavior and why? What could we start thinking and doing differently to contribute towards a change? This is not intended to suggest that we ignore corruption, but once we have identified the things that are rotten to the core then we can immediately set about transforming them and replacing them with something much more supportive to our communities. What if we started noticing and rewarding those in our society who are behaving in an exemplary manner and holding them up as a shining example, celebrating their honesty, dedication and transparency? What potential is there to inspire others, particularly young people, to emulate them? How, rather than focusing upon the negative, might we instead enable our societies to evolve and thrive? When we bounce thoughts and ideas off one another we often conjure up new ones, helping us co-create something far grander than we could ever have dreamed up alone.

Mirrors
The next time you find yourself irritated by someone in your entourage, ask yourself what is it about their behavior that you dislike. What is it that they are doing that you also do? What do they think or say that you also think or say? What do they mirror in yourself? Ask yourself why you behave in that way. What is the underlying fear? The answers will be very illuminating. Draw three columns on a sheet of paper. In the first, jot down what commonly-held thoughts or collective beliefs you notice around you. In the second column note how you think or behave in a similar way to that which you are jointly criticizing. In the final column list the ways in which you might be able to focus your thoughts differently. How can you contribute, even in a small way, to the positive transformation of those collective beliefs that are unsupportive? Change has to begin somewhere. It starts with us.

Our thoughts flow to us and through us just like the very air that we breathe. The majority of people misdirect the incredible power of thought, wasting vast amounts of energy as they do so, with aimless, indecisive, chaotic thinking. Our challenge is to constructively channel, focus and direct our thinking. That is where true mastery lies.

No person will ever manage to achieve perfection of thought, or anywhere close, nor will we ever be totally content with our current circumstances. We are progressive beings, designed to be constantly striving for more, growing, experiencing, and discovering our preferences. Strive then towards the ideal, and seek to uplift and ennoble that which already exists upon the earth.

Nowhere!
Not in the sky,
Nor in the midst of the sea,
Nor deep in the mountains,
Can you hide from your own mischief.
– **Buddha,** *Dhammapada*

Chapter 4

Limiting Beliefs

When I let go of what I am, I become who I might be.
– Lao Tzu

A belief is simply a thought that we keep thinking over and over again, reinforced by imagination and emotion. When we believe something the Universe will assist us to gather evidence which supports that belief, whether we are conscious of it or not. What we believe or judge in some way we claim for ourselves.

We hold literally thousands of beliefs about ourselves and others, both as individuals and collectively. They contribute to our sense of identity – what we consider to be our personality – and to what we think is possible or impossible, how we behave, what risks we are prepared to take, how we respond to others. We hold beliefs about our loved ones, about people we've never met, groups of people in society, organizations. Most importantly, we hold many beliefs about ourselves. We compare, measure and criticize ourselves constantly, against others and against the standards that we have set for ourselves in our minds. "This is who I am." "This is what I stand for." "This is what I believe to be right." "This is what I can do." "This is what I cannot do." "This is how I must behave in this situation." Some of these beliefs nurture and support us, while others are anchored in fear and keep us stuck, preventing us from moving forward and depleting our energy. Often our beliefs cause us to limit ourselves in some way, or to be actively aggressive towards ourselves. "I look awful," "I'm useless," "I'll never be good enough," "I'm always sick," "That person is better than me," "I'm no good at math," "Spiritual people shouldn't earn lots of money," "Healing has to be painful in order to be effective," we tell ourselves, or, "Why would anybody love me? I'm unlovable." Through our limiting beliefs we cut ourselves off from the stream of well-being that is constantly flowing to us.

Beliefs are simply our habitual ways of processing the world we see around us, the agreements we have made with ourselves that we have built up over the course of our lifetime. They are filters through which we regard life from our own unique perspective, ingrained patterns of thinking through which we ultimately create our reality. Astrologers notice how these filters are influenced by the position of the sun, the moon and the planets at the time we first emerge as souls onto this planet. Their angles to one another have the potential to affect the choices we make and the way we respond to our life experiences, as we each navigate through time and space. Kabbalists teach that the human is but a microcosm of something far greater, our body a miniature of the macrocosmic solar system.

That which is Above is like that which is Below and that which is Below is like that which is Above, to accomplish the Miracle of Unity.
– **Hermes Trismegistus**

Each of us is unique, and will react differently to life events depending upon the way that we perceive them. For example, although all the children in a household may experience the same conflictual relationship between their parents they will each respond to and interiorize the events in very different ways. Any difficulties they experience as a result will in large part be dependent upon the extent to which, both consciously and unconsciously, they feel affected by the events.

Our physical bodies are programmed to respond to our beliefs. Our muscles contract or relax and our breathing and posture change depending upon the belief we hold at any given moment. If we believe we are in danger we hold ourselves in a very different way than if we think we have done something to be ashamed of or if we feel a reason to be proud. In a precarious situation our body is flooded with chemicals and hormones such as adrenaline and cortisol, our heart races, we may start to sweat and our mouth may turn dry. The links between mind and body are astonishingly clear. Our cells are constantly listening and responding to what we tell them, so make sure you tell yours a story that is supportive.

Why do you believe the things you do? Where did these beliefs come from? Many of our beliefs are formed out of the beliefs of others. The spoken words and nonverbal behavior of our parents, teachers and friends, and the cultural expectations of the society we grow up in influence us greatly. Others become established through our life experiences. "Last time I did this that happened." "Every time I do that, such and such happens." We quickly learn that if we behave in a certain way we gain something, whether material reward or approval, and if we behave in another way we might lose something, feel pain or be punished in some way.

Our unconscious mind does not indiscriminately absorb all beliefs that come its way. We are not left totally defenseless, entirely subject to the thoughts of others. Each belief is first filtered through the conscious mind, enabling us to accept or reject it as we choose. Only those beliefs that we *accept* are subsequently assimilated into the role we assume for ourselves. Once we hold a certain belief we are automatically predisposed to accepting similar beliefs from others.

Believe nothing, no matter where you read it or who has said it, not even if I have said it, unless it agrees with your own reason and your own common sense.
– **Buddha**

There is an old Zen story about a powerful, magnificent lion who was brought up in a herd of sheep. All his life he believed himself to be a sheep, behaving exactly as they did, until one day he was captured by an old lion who showed him his reflection in the water of a pond. So many of us suppress our uniqueness in a similar way. We don't recognize our own majesty or prowess. Instead, we think and behave like sheep instead of truly being ourselves. Rather than gaining a better understanding of who and what we really are, and having the courage to reveal it to others, we conform to the expectations of the community with which we have surrounded ourselves.

We are not responsible for the beliefs of others. A woman's parents may be unhappy that their daughter is leaving a dysfunctional and violent relationship, while living in a society in which cultural norms dictate that women should remain married to the same partner for life. It is the parents' beliefs about the situation that have caused their unhappiness, not the actions of their daughter. In another culture the same parents might be relieved that she has finally seen sense and is no longer putting herself in danger. It is not our role to police the beliefs of others. Indeed, it is futile to try to do so, and will usually result in avoidable conflict. As tempting as it may be to blame others for their reactions and beliefs, true self-mastery requires that the focus remains on understanding ourselves better. Take the opportunity to practice allowing others to have their own learning experiences without interfering.

One who understands others has knowledge;
One who understands himself has wisdom.
Mastering others requires force;
Mastering the self needs strength.
– Lao Tzu

A core belief is a particularly strong idea we hold about our own existence, and becomes invisible when we take it to be a given fact.

Once we believe something to be true it will keep proving itself to be true until we change what we believe. If we want to thrive and live a vital and healthy life then self-knowledge is absolutely essential. We must make genuine efforts to become familiar with our subconscious thoughts and the stories we tell ourselves. When we let go of our beliefs we also inevitably release many of our expectations about how people should behave or what should happen next. In so doing we save ourselves from a great deal of suffering.

Once we become aware of our beliefs then we can build upon those that are positive and adapt those that are unsupportive. As we begin to recognize our core beliefs we start to realize that they are simply points of view or opinions. They are not something absolute. Once we understand this it becomes much easier to set about their transformation. As we recognize those core beliefs that are false, we can choose to release or change them. Other beliefs that are linked to them will also fall away automatically, and all the power with which they were created returns to us. We free up mental space within which we can create a new perspective, and through which energy can flow freely. We can begin to create new neural pathways, new response patterns and behaviors. In effect, we build a new identity.

If you do not like the effects of a belief you must alter it, for no manipulation of the exterior conditions themselves will release you.
– Seth, channeled via Jane Roberts

Question
Ask yourself, "Who am I?" Paint a picture of yourself
with core statements as you envisage yourself today.
Use the labels you ascribe to yourself on a regular basis.
Describe yourself in terms such as 'I am a teacher', 'I
am a bank manager', 'I am a scientist', 'I am a mother',
'I am a son', 'I am a wife', 'I am a lover', 'I am good

at skiing', 'I am sociable', 'I am stressed', 'I am sick',
'I am a Taurus', 'I am broke', 'I am an animal-lover',
'I am optimistic', 'I am Catholic', 'I am careful', 'I am
a conservative', 'I am someone who believes...', 'I am
practical', 'I am fat', 'I am always late', 'I am no good
at remembering names', 'I am loyal', 'I am creative', 'I
am flexible'. Carefully note your perceived qualities and
flaws. Do they accurately reflect who you aspire to be?

These beliefs about yourself determine the choices that are open
to you, and what you do with your life. If you believe yourself to
be shy, you are unlikely to pursue a career in public speaking or
the performance arts, even if you have an exceptional talent for
it. If you think you are no good at school then you may opt not to
pursue a course of further education that could open the route to
the career you dream of. How do these statements support your
ambitions in life? Are you happy? Have you realized all your
dreams and goals? How do those beliefs restrict and limit you?
Our task, then, is to ascertain who we really are, on a much deeper
level, and to decide who we choose to be from this point forward.

As you think, so shall you become.
– **Bruce Lee**

Take a close look at your life. Scrutinize every aspect of it closely;
your home, your relationships, your career, your health, your
financial circumstances. You will find that each area is directly
reflecting what you have been telling yourself about it. Remember,
your current life experience is just a result of your previous
thinking, and you can change your thoughts at any moment. If
your beliefs are not enabling you to experience life in the way that
you wish, then it is essential that you set about changing them.

Does what you believe pertain to the current situation, or is
your belief based upon something that happened previously?

Just because you were rejected in the last job interview, it doesn't mean that this prospective employer won't absolutely love you. Is the person you are in conversation with really not paying attention or are you bristling with irritation just because they didn't listen properly to you the last time you met?

Are you making assumptions? If an art gallery decides not to display your work, perhaps your art simply isn't right for the feel of that particular exhibition. It doesn't mean that your art has no value. A gentle folk singer is not usually the best fit for a heavy metal band. Just because someone can't bellow out gospel or rock and roll it doesn't mean their voice is not hauntingly beautiful. A knock-back might not be a sign that someone should stop singing, but maybe that they would be better as a solo performer, collaborating with a different combination of musicians or performing in front of a different audience at another venue. We self-sabotage so often because we make assumptions about what others believe about us, when really, we are afraid that we fall short in some way. We use these beliefs against ourselves. Time and again we hurt ourselves with our assumptions about what others believe about us, using them as an excuse for not trying in case we fail.

If you hear a voice within you say, "You cannot paint," then by all means paint, and that voice will be silenced.
– **Vincent van Gogh**

Each limiting belief must be identified and pulled out one by one. It is not enough to cast it to one side, and decide not to look at it anymore. Further layers of beliefs will accumulate around it, thus increasing its power. Ignoring something will merely repress it. Ultimately it will gain strength under pressure until at some point it will burst to the surface again, propelled by emotion, and often exposed in an extreme way. Nature will leave no space unfilled, so we use this principle to our advantage. As each belief is identified, we can also identify its opposite and begin to embed new thought patterns that are more aligned to our true nature. As we do so, these thoughts will attract others of a similar nature and the new belief will grow in strength.

So how do we set about installing and activating new beliefs? First we have to identify the replacement thought, and then we need to accept it as a potential in our life. Even if we have absolutely no idea how it might become a reality given the current circumstances in front of us, we allow the idea that the possibility for change exists in *every* situation to permeate us. Do not reject the current experience, simply allow it to be present, appreciating the insight it has to offer. It is just holding up a mirror to our past thinking. Remain steady in the understanding that an alternative already exists in vibrational form. In just the same way that we formed the original belief by repeatedly thinking the same thought over and over again, so we can ingrain a new belief by consciously selecting and repeating a different message. This is why repeating affirmations can be so powerful, provided that they are *heartfelt*.

Beliefs do not operate in isolation from imagination and emotion so we allow ourselves to consider what it might be like if the new belief were actually present in our reality. We focus our attention on the potential that has yet to physically manifest. What might it look like? How does it make us feel? How would we behave differently? We use what we know about others to inform ourselves. If, for example, our desire is to feel financially secure or to become a confident public speaker, then we ask ourselves how someone who has those qualities might behave. In what ways does our behavior usually differ? This does not mean that we should imitate others but gentle comparison can shed light upon our expectations and underlying beliefs. Successful people often achieve great things precisely because they have been successful on many previous occasions. They expect things to go well. What are you expecting the outcome to be? Self-assured people hold themselves upright and speak convincingly. They look you directly in the eye. How do you hold yourself? Confidence can be gained by something as simple as holding ourselves with a confident posture.

Be true to yourself, rather than replicating what others are doing. It is impossible for anyone else to define you. Instead, use the success of those who you find inspiring to gain insight and self-knowledge.

To be yourself in a world that is constantly trying to make you something else is the greatest accomplishment.
– Ralph Waldo Emerson

Don't beat yourself up if the ego tells you that you are somehow falling short, which it surely will. Each and every one of us feels insecure in some way, even the most accomplished. "It's been done before," "It's nothing new," "You'll never pull it off," "You're too old," that relentless inner critic drones on. While we are worrying about what people think of us, in our strange, narcissistic way, the truth is that most people aren't thinking about us at all. Unless it affects them personally, what we look like and how we perform is of little importance to others. None of us is perfect. It is part of our intrinsic nature to continually be seeking to improve and evolve, eternally looking for better.

Be prepared to give up the belief that something isn't possible and have the courage to take risks. The greatest endeavors, explorations and innovations involve an element of risk.

Don't be satisfied with stories, how things have gone with others. Unfold your own myth.
– Rumi

Refuse to take things personally. If someone is laughing hysterically at an unkind comment they have made, even if it holds a grain of truth, ask yourself whether they are laughing because their joke is funny, or because it has made them feel more powerful. How insecure must they be feeling to need to reassure themselves in this way? Maybe their words are like a torch shining upon a deeper hurt. Question yourself, challenge yourself to see what's really going on beneath the surface, and be grateful for the clarity they are providing. Perhaps you were the one doing the laughing?

Frequently our desires do not stem from something we want to be, to do or to have, as might seem to be the case at first glance, but from our expectations. We desire something because we think that when we have it we will feel a certain way. We want to create a certain feeling state. It is important to examine what we believe about ourselves that prevents us from feeling that way right now. What is the belief that is holding us back? For example, we may want to have more money because we feel that we can't do the things we want to do without it. We might want to explore, go on adventures, learn new things or meet inspiring people. When we look more closely we may see that it is not more money that we truly desire, but more freedom, more expansion or more opportunities to create. The money is merely a means to an end.

Some hold the belief that rich people are greedy, and that it's wrong to be wealthy and spiritual. Money is just a form of energy, like any other. It is what we intend to do with it that is of importance. It's not necessary to deprive ourselves of material things in order to achieve spiritual attainment. Embodied spirituality is where it's at.

Solomon, with all his wealth, was no less wise.
– **Hazrat Inayat Khan**

There is absolutely no reason why someone should not be able to earn their living helping others or why someone who truly loves their work, such as an artist or musician, should not be paid for the pleasure their work gives others. The words of Frans Stiene, senior teacher at the International House of Reiki, in a Facebook thread resonated strongly with me:

> *Water is free, but if you want it in your house you may need to pay a plumber.*

Perhaps we believe that there will not be enough to go around, or if we have something someone else must go without. Examine the truth of these assumptions. Do others become well when we deprive ourselves of health?

We may hold competing beliefs. If, for example, we are sick and exploring holistic options but we hold the belief that we will only get better if we take medicine, then we might be better to get a prescription from the doctor rather than by trying to heal ourselves through thought alone.

On further examining our beliefs we may find that we currently feel stuck and contracted or bored and restless. We may be telling ourselves 'I can't' in some way. We gain a closer insight as to the belief or beliefs that are out of alignment with our soul state, and which are causing us the discomfort. Once we have identified the way we really want to feel, then we can look for more opportunities in our lives to replicate that feeling state. The likelihood is that we will be able to find many opportunities each day to feel a certain way. If we find ourselves craving freedom and fresh experiences, we might buy a map and take a walk along a track that we have never investigated before, or shop in a different town. We might create a piece of art using a technique we've never tried, or learn a musical instrument. We could challenge and stretch our bodies in new ways, and take up a physical activity we've not tried before. We might try a new meditation technique, develop a lucid dreaming practice or simply change our day-to-day routine. We shake things up a bit, break out of our comfort zone.

We might long for a relationship with someone new. Why is that? What will that person bring that we don't already have? Do we believe they will inspire us, motivate us, or challenge us in some way? Is it safety we crave? Companionship? Practical support? Delirious sex? Meaningful conversation? What are the sensations that those things bring? How can we create more of them for ourselves without the longed-for partner? Perhaps there is something we believe about ourselves that is creating a barrier. Do we feel we will only attract someone if we look a certain way? If we lose weight, buy that new dress, get a new haircut or become more cultured. What do we currently feel about ourselves? Do we recognize ourselves as the magnificent beings that we truly are, or do we feel small and less than, not good enough? What are the qualities we are seeking in another person that we are unable to see in ourselves?

How many of us know we are fed up to the back teeth of working in the same old job, day in, day out, or are frustrated by a lack of promotion or other such recognition? And how many of us who this applies to know what we'd really like to do instead? There are so many possibilities that the choice can be overwhelming, so we stay in the safe zone and make no changes. We wait for the outer circumstances to change, rather than making radical inner changes. Instead of asking, "What could I do for a living?" try asking questions such as, "How do I want to feel?" and "How can I be of most service?"

Challenge yourself, dig deep and you will surely find hidden treasure. Ask yourself where the beliefs you hold come from. More importantly, ask yourself if they are true. What does your soul know? How does what you think differ? Dig even more deeply and you will almost certainly begin to realize that your restlessness and dissatisfaction stem from something far more profound.

Our real self, the spirit, is ever perfect and free. But we have forgotten that. So we identify with our present experience of bondage and consequently suffer in countless ways. Our situation is like someone who is asleep and dreaming that he is being tortured and beaten. In reality he is not being touched at all; yet he is experiencing very real pain and fear. He need not placate, overpower, or escape his torturers. He needs only to wake up.
– **Swami Nirmalananda (Abbot George Burke)**

One Hundred Things

A great exercise to help us establish what we are really itching to achieve in life is to make a bucket list of 25 things we wish to be, do or have. Then write down a further 25, repeating this process twice more, so that eventually the list contains 100 items. What places would you like to visit? What adventures do you dream of having? What would you like to learn or improve? How might you develop yourself? What health goals do you have? How could you improve your career? Your finances? Your relationships? What can you contribute to others, to your community? How can you challenge yourself? What would you find fun? We often get so bogged down in day-to-day living that we lose a sense of perspective about what really matters to us. Don't wait for a dramatic wake-up call before deciding not to waste another second of your life. Give yourself permission to consider what really matters to you.

At first the exercise is relatively easy, but as it progresses we often find ourselves struggling for things to put on the list. It's entirely possible that at some point desires that we have put on the back burner or had subconsciously written off as being unachievable or 'silly' will emerge.

Now, pair each item on the list with the one below

it. Very quickly, without allowing the mind time to intervene, select just one item on the list, and erase the other. Work your way through the list until you reach the bottom. Put the remaining desires into pairs and repeat the exercise. Continue in this way until only one thing is left on the list. Don't worry, it's only an exercise. It won't prevent you from going to a place you've always longed to visit *and* having a fulfilling career. However, there is a strong likelihood that at times you will find yourself screaming inwardly, "Nooooo, I can't possibly cross that off the list, it's too important to me." Familiarity with our real priorities is valuable self-knowledge indeed.

Know thyself.
– **Ancient Greek aphorism**

Chapter 5

The Word

The knower of the mystery of sound knows the mystery of the whole universe.
– Hazrat Inayat Khan

If our thoughts are the means by which a creation is set into motion, then our words are the mechanism by which we bring it into physicality. We humans are unique on this planet in that we have the ability to form words, with which we can shape our reality. Every word we speak, every sentence we utter is a thread that we weave into the fabric of our lives.

When we speak we move air, which vibrates as the words leave our mouths and travel out into the atmosphere, changing the form of the air as they do so. We can easily see the effects when we talk outside on a cold winter's day, or when we speak very close to a water surface. Thanks to technological advances, the emerging science of cymatics now enables us to render visible sound frequencies and vibrations that would ordinarily pass unseen. The vibrations make complex geometric patterns upon the surface of a sensitive water membrane, which can be filmed and the resulting images can then be examined closely. This provides rich food for thought if we consider the percentage of water molecules in our bodies. From these studies we can see that every sound we make – the words we utter, even the voices of things that are usually inaudible to the human ear, such as cells and stars – creates an intricately detailed, dynamic geometric pattern. This exciting young science offers many insights into some of our most profound questions about the formation of matter and the nature of physical reality.

Many say that life entered the human body by the help of music, but the truth is that life itself is music.
– **Hafiz**

Sound is simply the transfer of vibrations between atoms or molecules 'bumping into' one another. When an object vibrates it causes air particles to move so that they collide with the air particles next to them. This makes the adjacent particles vibrate and they, in turn, bump into other particles. The faster the vibration, the higher the frequency and the corresponding musical note that is produced. The human voice contains many complex sound frequencies. In the virtual vacuum of space, where there are no air molecules to bump into, 'sound' exists in the form of electromagnetic vibrations pulsating in various wavelengths.

Contrary to popular belief, sound doesn't move in a linear way, but in a spherical form. Think of the rings that are produced when you throw a stone into a pond, but imagine them instead as a beautiful, expanding, rhythmically pulsating 3D bubble. Sound travels much faster through water than it does through air. To what extent do our words and thoughts affect our cellular structure?

Our cells may not have ears, in the sense that we understand them, but they are nevertheless listening and responding to every word we say. Every vowel has a significance, every consonant has its effect, and the composition of each word spoken has both a psychological and a chemical significance. There are delicate nerve centers throughout the human body upon which mental and physical well-being depend that are easily affected by vibration. Each word spoken has the potential to affect both body and mind. The Word is more than just a language. It is also a science. Ponder this deeply.

Behind the breath there lies a much finer, often imperceptible, spiritual component. This spiritual breath has the properties of an electric current and vibrates internally. On the face of it the spoken word is a physical phenomenon in which sound is produced via the body, through the action of the lungs, diaphragm, and mouth etc., but when we consider sound more closely we realize that it is impossible to speak or sing without first thinking. We often feel the emotion of what we are about to say long before the words have even left our lips. While there is a physical aspect to the words we speak they are, in effect, generated by the soul, vibrating first through our heart and our mind.

Just as our thoughts are every bit as real as something that is visible and touchable within the material world, so is the spoken word. The Word is an expressive manifestation of the breath, of vital life force itself, and operates with astonishing power within the domain of medium gross matter. It brings the spiritual into the manifest world and is a blueprint for creation. It pays to consider the words we choose very carefully.

All of the mystical teachings make reference to the power of the Word, but over the years the sense of the texts have much evolved, with many subtle and not so subtle changes due to translation and the fashion of the day. In many cases the original meaning has been lost and it can be most helpful to examine the ancient teachings closely so as to obtain a more accurate idea of what was being conveyed. The early Gnostics held the Gospel of John to be of great significance. In it, John wrote:

In the beginning was the Word, and the Word was with God, and the Word was God. He was with God in the beginning. Through him all things were made; without him nothing was made that has been made. In him was life, and that life was the light of men.
– John 1.1–4

Notice that this paragraph didn't say "some things". It said "*all* things" were made. That's a pretty powerful creative force. This tells us clearly that the Word underpins all that is in existence.

In this case, "Word" is a translation of the Greek word *'logos'* meaning not only 'word, speech, statement and discourse' but also 'computation, account, reason, to collect, to gather, expectation, plea, ground'. Heraclitus (c. 535–475 BCE) used it to describe 'a principle of order and knowledge'. Stoic philosophers identified it as 'the divine animating principle pervading the Universe'. Philo and Plato referred to it not only as the spoken word, but also as the word still in the mind, acting as an intermediary between the realms of form and the formless. Today, the *Encyclopedia Britannica* describes the *'logos'* as "the divine reason implicit in the cosmos, ordering it and giving it form and meaning". Something that is implicit is integral to the nature or essence of something but is unexpressed, not revealed or developed. From this we get a sense that, even if the sounds themselves are discreet, the Word drives the formation of all the structures in our physical world, is continually evolving and has intelligent, conscious attributes. Indeed, some might say that it is the mechanism of consciousness itself.

The teachings of Philo held the creative Source to be intangible, imperceptible, with no attributes, existing beyond time and space, whereas the logos acts both as a bridge for the Divine mind and a sort of cosmic glue, holding matter together.

The Logos of the living God is the bond of everything, holding all things together and binding all the parts, and prevents them from being dissolved and separated.
– Philo

Whereas the Source is still, formless, unchanging and cannot be associated with any place, the Logos has form and implies motion from place to place. Through the actions of the Logos, fine gross matter (thought) and medium gross matter (the spoken word) make their way into the visible, material world (dense gross matter), in accordance with the universal law of vibration.

And the Word was made flesh, and dwelt among us.
– **John 1.14**

In obedience to the law,
The word of the Master grew into flower.
– **Hermes Trismegistus, *The Emerald Tablets of Thoth***

I am the Word. The Word I am.
– **A channeled teaching through Paul Selig**

What you speak, you claim. Let the significance of this sink in for a moment. What words do you repeatedly choose to speak about yourself? Not only do our words affect our personal reality but they also have a considerable influence upon those we speak about. Does what you say about others pull them down, making them feel heavy and worthless? Why you would choose to do that? Does it perhaps make you feel bigger, better or more important? Do your words injure, or do you choose words that support, uplift and inspire?

The choice of words is a serious business, and with them come great responsibility. It is no coincidence that words have an important role to play in mystical and spiritual rituals the world over, through the use of mantras, jumon, spells and incantations. Sometimes referred to as kotodama, the power of spirit is inherent in all vocalized sounds, within the very breath and the heart of them. When we verbalize something, it is as if we place an order with the impartial Universe, which will generously deliver whatever we have requested, whether we have done so consciously or otherwise. To engage in 'kotage' is to engage in the manipulation of cosmic forces. In this world of duality, there are two sides to everything in existence. With our words we can call into being the most beautiful experience or we can create or prolong a miserable situation. We can build and enhance or we can damage and destroy. When speaking, it pays to be very clear about the sorts of things we would like to experience and to bring into our lives.

Be impeccable with your word.
– Don Miguel Ruiz

How many people today truly stop to think about what they are saying? Consider the damage that careless words can cause. Not only is the placebo effect very real, so too is that of the nocebo. The words we use are like seeds that we sow in the minds of others. Any medical professional or healer worth their salt will tell you how important it is that they use language that soothes and supports their client, rather than filling them with fear. My own grandfather was told by his doctor that he "probably had around six months to live" and died within six months of that diagnosis. I know numerous others who have had a similar prognosis but, having heard very different words from their support team, go on to live happy and healthy lives for many years to come.

How often do you tell yourself, "I have...", and you fill in the blanks and give it a name? Rest assured that your body heard every word and will respond accordingly, nourishing still further the dis-ease or the problem you just claimed for yourself. Try regularly telling your body a different story, and watch and see what gets delivered instead. If only the pessimist understood the potentially destructive power of their self-talk.

Each atom and molecule in the body, each organ, has a sound value and a frequency which is not heard externally, expressing themselves instead as inner sounds. When something is out of balance these sounds become discordant and inharmonious. Our words and thoughts have considerable influence upon these inner sounds and can bring them back into harmony, or can create further discord. It is of vital importance that we do not further reinforce unsupportive beliefs with negative self-talk or assumptions about the condition of others. It also explains why things such as chanting, toning, tuning forks, gongs and Tibetan bowls can have such a powerful effect upon the body.

Are you one of those people who loves to respond to a simple 'How are you?' by outlining the details of every challenge or problem in your life? The Universal laws automatically apply as equally to such words as they do to the words of those who are conscious and careful about what they are propagating. "Poor me," we wail, "Poor me." And of course, misery loves company, so we will inevitably find more than ample opportunity to reinforce our beliefs about whatever situation we happen to find ourselves struggling with. At times, the pity parties become competitive, with each participant trying to outdo each other in their suffering. "What I'm going through is so much worse," "Look at me, look at me. Look how much pain I'm in," the ego will cry, and, in complete ignorance of the Universal laws, we go and repeat the unformed words in our heads right out loud. And what do you think we experience as a result? What do you tell others, over and over again? What do you tell your innate? Well done. You've just owned it. Every word that is spoken acts upon multiple planes of existence, affecting mind, body and spirit.

> *Even in pain, if a person could refrain from saying: "I am in pain,"*
> *he would do a great deal of good to himself.*
> **- Hazrat Inayat Khan**

Imagine, for a few moments, your life as a movie. The film appears to flow continuously but in fact it is made up of numerous individual frames that appear in sequence. If you keep on putting frames into your movie that contain problems, disease and difficult situations, then that is what will appear on the screen. If you continuously insert a similar looking and sounding frame then the film will appear as though it is unchanged. However, if you were to insert a different frame or frames the story has the potential to develop in a completely different way. You can't have happy endings if you keep acting out bleak, gloomy, miserable or terrifying scripts. Instead, why not start telling yourself how magnificent you are, how dazzlingly well you feel, how much you appreciate all that life has to offer, and see how your story develops? Before you speak out loud, stop for a second and take a deep breath. Take the time to tune into your innate. Do the words you are about to say soothe or do they incite? How do they feel in your body? Do they make you feel heavy, or do they feel light and expansive? Could you write a better story? If you're not sure how, then ask your innate to help you to find the right words and be patient. Allow some time to pass before you write the next scene.

The wise man lets his heart overflow but keeps silent his mouth.
– The Emerald Tablets of Thoth the Atlantean

Whenever we thoughtlessly speak cruel and vicious words about ourselves or others, we are inadvertently using black magick. We spread poison. We inspire hatred, particularly towards those we perceive as being different from ourselves, or who hold a different perspective to us: different races, ethnic groups and cultures, political parties, religions, tribes, countries. We divide, we separate. We measure ourselves against others, deeming some as 'better than' and others to be 'less worthy', oblivious of the power of our words. Communication breaks down. Our words are often full of envy or resentment, even within our own families. Especially within our own families. We gossip. We cause chaos.

Not that which goeth into the mouth defileth a man; but that which cometh out of the mouth, this defileth a man.
– Matthew 15.11

Over the years gossip has become a cultural norm. Our newspapers, television screens and social media are full of it. Intentional use of gossip is a recognized strategy. In marketing it can be used to build or break a brand, and in the world of Intelligence 'dissemination' and 'disinformation' are valuable tools indeed. We love nothing more than to share our opinion about everyone we know, even about those we've never met. It's what we *'do'* when we gather with friends and family, and we learn the habit at a very young age. It is a habit worthy of transformation.

In my classes I often share an exercise in which we measure the electromagnetic field or 'aura' of a person, and then we watch to see how it is influenced by thinking happy, sad, angry or fearful thoughts. We watch again to understand how someone's field is influenced by another person's thoughts. I can assure you, nothing makes an energy field contract more quickly than the unkind words of a group of people. There is an upside to this. A group of people talking affectionately about someone causes their field to expand dramatically. Think back to the last time someone told you that you looked fabulous, or congratulated you for a job well done. Think about someone you love. My guess is that you grew taller and more upright just thinking about these things. When we feel good our chests expand, we breathe differently, our energy field expands, our posture and facial expressions change; we literally feel lighter and happier. We feel energized, and we have more energy to share with others. Can you remember going to a great party or music festival? When a group of people are bouncing off each other joyfully, the energy is palpable.

The wonder of being human is that we always have free choice. Instead of focusing upon the unwanted, choose words that come from the heart, and speak with kindness and love. As we practice using words of compassion and integrity, we attract more thoughts and experiences that resonate with them. We align ourselves to a higher consciousness, and in so doing leave less room in the mind for that which does not fully support us. Start paying attention to the creations that result from your words, wanted and unwanted, and take responsibility for the words which come from your mouth.

Most of us speak primarily from our heads, from the logical, intellectual, analytical mind. We give voice to the ego, so deeply invested in feeling insecure. Such words are far less powerful than the Word that is spoken from the heart. Words from the head are quickly forgotten. Words from the heart remain with us for years. If you're in any doubt of this, just look at the impact made by the passionate words shared by people such as Martin Luther King Jr., Maya Angelou, and John Lennon. Fill your words with love. Speak from your heart and you will touch the hearts of others.

When thoughts and feelings are put into words they instantly become more powerful. Have you ever felt really sad yet managed to keep your emotions under control, only to find that as soon as you started to speak you were unable to stop the tears? Have you felt anger and resentment building inside until finally your words erupted in a verbally violent confrontation? How did your physical posture change? Your whole way of being?

The emotional force that propels the word into expression has a great deal of influence upon how the word is perceived by the listener. Words of truth and sincerity have considerably more force than those that are inauthentic. When someone is lying you can both hear and feel it. The spoken word is weaker, and its vibration feels 'off'. Their words don't 'ring true'. The voice of someone who has no confidence in themselves will never inspire confidence in another. The words of the shop assistant who says 'thank you' unthinkingly numerous times throughout the day will have far less impact than the 'Thank you,' 'Yes! Get in!' or 'Halleluiah' of the person who is genuinely grateful. Feel the truth and the wisdom that emanate from the words passed down from generation to generation by indigenous elders. When someone speaks with conviction their words penetrate deeply.

When a thought pops into your head, give it time to mature

before speaking it out loud. It will condense as it is held in silence, just as steam does in a pressure cooker, and become more powerful. Pressure and condensation significantly influence the qualities of magnetic activity, and, in the same way that homogenous species are drawn together on the physical plane, like thoughts will attract like thoughts and the thought will gain more power. Be sure to wait until the appropriate words have been formulated in your head before speaking them. Once a word has been spoken it cannot be taken back. The laws of the Universe apply unfailingly and there will be an effect on some level, albeit there are a variety of things that influence the eventual outcome. You may hold a stone in your hand for as long as you like. You can take aim, you can decide how much force you are going to use. But once the stone has left your hand it is going to fly regardless, according to the direction and the amount of force used. No amount of other stones will call that stone back. It is possible to amass a big pile of stones in another place subsequently, but the first stone will still lie exactly where it landed until it is moved or the structure of it is altered in some other way. Forms may change. The power of the original Word remains, eternal and indestructible.

The spoken word is audible, and frequently has a visible effect, but it is *realized* within. Words can provide clarity or they can cause confusion. Words have the ability to make us feel something, they inspire us to take action. Tactless words can offend and incite an aggressive or even violent response. Foolish words spoken without thought can prove to be extremely disadvantageous. Some words are a blessing, giving comfort and reassurance or bringing healing. Others provide courage and strength. Others still are sacred, and have mystical powers reaching way beyond the physical plane.

Be mindful of words that block energy flow. You may begin to speak and create with a sentence that is spiritually inspired, only to considerably dilute, redirect or delay its effect with words that stem from the ego. Such words are usually based in fear or reflect a lack of self-worth. The word *'but'* is a great example of such a word. "I would go traveling but...", "I would apply for that job I dream of but...", "I would introduce myself to that person who I'd love to get to know better but..." When you notice yourself using such a word, examine your thoughts and feelings closely. Ask yourself, "What is the self-doubt?" "Why am I stalling?" "I'm afraid," "I'm not good enough," "It won't make any difference," says the ego. What does the soul say?

Our words gain power when they are repeated. If someone tells you you're stupid or no good at something often enough, after a while, you will start to believe them. For this very reason, positive affirmations can be a great way of reinforcing supportive belief systems and reprogramming neural networks. In Buddhist, Hindu, Jewish, Muslim, Zoroastrian and Catholic traditions the same sounds, syllables, words and phrases are repeated over and over, in the understanding that, when used correctly, repetition can be a powerful tool for the raising of consciousness. In the East, gurus and murshids will often prescribe a certain word or phrase to be repeated in order to alleviate physical, mental or emotional suffering, or to help someone to attain a particular goal.

The words we use every day not only have a psychological significance but they also have a numerical and astrological value. These are vast subjects which impact upon every other existing art and science, and are beyond the scope of this book. Suffice to say that the mystical word has an even greater value than the words we use day to day. Certain words invoke particular planets, either diminishing or increasing their influence. In many traditions a person is named in accordance with astrological calculations. The name a person is given can have a great effect upon their life and career.

The word that is in existence cannot be lost, but many are

those who have lost their ability to hear it. The art of listening is worth cultivating, and in doing so we should ensure that we are listening to the voice that emanates from the earth herself. While the human word only affects the planes of fine gross matter, it nevertheless holds the potential to affect everything earthly. It has the power to retroactively affect the lives and futures of those upon the planet.

The words you speak become the house you live in.
– Hafiz

Chapter 6

Emotion

Love is not an emotion. It is your very existence.
– **Sri Sri Ravi Shankar**

If thought is the mechanism which drives our creations, then emotions provide the fuel by which they are propelled. Based upon French and Latin words meaning to 'excite, stir up, agitate, move out, move away', the word *'e-motion'* in itself suggests movement. Emotions can dramatically influence the speed with which something manifests into physical reality. Sometimes it is wise to take our foot off the accelerator, slowing down and enjoying the ride, appreciating the view as we journey through life. On other occasions a little more oomph is called for, some extra impetus. When we feel something strongly it's like plugging our thoughts and our words into a big set of stereo speakers. They are amplified. They gain power. Emotions propel our thoughts from the nonphysical to the physical, and the intensity of our feeling, the force with which we feel, is a critical element in their subsequent manifestation.

Our thoughts, actions, feeling and physiology are inextricably connected. For every thought we have, both conscious and unconscious, a reciprocal feeling is inevitably generated. Every thought that we think causes us to feel a certain way, and thus one emotion will always be present, even if we are not overtly aware of it. Our emotions are in a perpetual state of flux, constantly changing. One emotion will always replace another. As drivers, when we turn the steering wheel of a car we make a choice, and even a slight change of direction has the potential to take us to a completely different place. A change of thought has the same effect and will bring about a corresponding change of emotion, and as we have already seen, we always have the ability to change our thoughts. As we think, so we feel.

Our conscious thinking largely determines our feelings and emotions, according to the beliefs that we hold, not the other way around. A long period of depression does not simply arise out of the blue, but rather as a result of entertaining negative or unsupportive beliefs over a period of time, which in turn generates feelings of despondency. If we have a deep-held belief that we are unworthy of happiness then no amount of personal willpower will cause us to feel happy. Instead, we must first come to grips with our underlying beliefs about our worthiness.

Not only do emotions provide fuel for our thoughts, but they also act as a sort of inner GPS, indicating the extent to which we are in alignment with our Higher nature. Our real selves, our spiritual selves, knowing the truth of what is, vibrate at a certain rate. Our physical selves vibrate at another. The difference between the two rates of vibration helps us feel the extent to which we are in or out of alignment and our bodies communicate this state of alignment to us. Our feelings of discomfort indicate the difference, the gap, between the source of well-being, what is good for us, and where our attention is currently focused. When we are out of alignment we feel a discord in our bodies. Humans are designed in such a way that we find it difficult to tolerate discord for any length of time. It is our nature to seek harmony. How often have you winced at the sounds of nails on a blackboard, or at a note that's off-key? Emotional discord, if ignored, may present in the form of dis-ease, and we might also feel pain, contraction or heaviness. Gravity operates within the subtle realms just as it does within the physical. We 'feel down'. When we are in resonance with our True selves then we feel a sense of harmony, balance, wellness, lightness of being, a feeling of expansion. Our emotions never betray us. Learn to pay attention to them and to ask questions each time you notice an uncomfortable feeling in your body. Listen to your self-talk.

The chances are you'll be able to say, "Ah, there's another story I keep telling myself that no longer aligns to who I now choose to be."

Anxiety, fear and pain are very useful responses, without which the human race would probably not have been able to survive. Automatic, extremely rapid, and often unconscious responses avert us to danger, forewarn us and prepare us for any action that may be necessary. If you inadvertently put your hand on a flame the pain will cause you to snatch your hand away. You won't think about it first, you will simply react. This is a wonderful mechanism indeed, because putting your hand on a flame is generally not particularly healthy for your body.

Studies have shown that cells in a petri dish will instinctively move away from toxins, yet move towards a form of nourishment, just as plants will gravitate towards light and tree roots will seek out water. The same is true for us. Our emotions are intended to encourage us to move towards those things that nurture and sustain us, and to recoil from those things that do us harm.

Experience
If you are unsure of the truth of this, just stand with your eyes shut for a few minutes until you find your center of balance. Think of something that feels really good - a time you felt intense love, a moment when you felt deeply relaxed and joyful, something that particularly inspired you or an important achievement for example. You will most likely notice that you sway slightly forwards. Equally, when you think of something that makes you feel sad or afraid you will almost certainly notice that your body rocks backwards slightly. Sometimes the movement is barely perceptible, but often the shift is blatant.
Now recreate the same thoughts but this time ask

yourself, "How does this feel in my body?" "Does it feel heavy or light?" "Do I feel invigorated or weary?" "Am I holding tension anywhere?" Perhaps you feel an energy flow, such as a buzz, a pulsing, a vibration, a tingle or a rush of elation. Do you have goose bumps? I call mine "truth bumps"; they are my inner "Yes!" If you are more visual try shutting your eyes. Perhaps a color comes to mind. Is it bright and vibrant or is it murky and somber?

If you cannot find it in your own body where will you go in search of it?
— **The Upanishads**

Our bodies are constantly transmitting information to us, but the majority of us have forgotten how to listen. Focusing on what they have to share allows us to step out of a pure response mode and into the role of a detached and curious observer. Next time you reach a choice point and have a decision to make, no matter how big or small, ask yourself, "How does this feel?", "Is this good for me?" and listen to the response. If you feel discomfort then question why it is present. Is it because you intuitively sense a situation is not in your best interests, or is it because of an underlying belief or thought pattern that does not support you? Is it true? Questions such as: "What is the emotion that is present?", "Why do I believe that?" and "Where does this belief come from?" can yield fascinating insights. Your body will never let you down. Pay attention to what it has to share. We are hardwired not only to survive, but to thrive.

When we generate a feeling state we create electrical and magnetic waves inside and beyond our bodies, which extend far into the world around us – not just a couple of meters, but many kilometers beyond the location of our physical heart. Our imagined, interior world elicits the same sort of emotional responses within our energy field as any real and present situation, causing it to contract or expand accordingly. This contraction and expansion of our electromagnetic field can be easily dowsed with a rod by even the most novice of dowsers, and provides a wonderfully visual demonstration of how our thoughts and emotions affect us. When we think positive, life-enhancing, joyful or loving thoughts our energy field expands, and when we think thoughts that originate in fear then it contracts, often dramatically.

Music and smell have the potential to trigger memories, both good and bad. Countless people associate the smell of disinfectant with sickness, hospitals and even death, and all the emotions that such things bring. I adore the smell of horses and damp leather, a reminder of many happy hours spent in their companionship while growing up. Even the smell of muckheaps can make me smile. A cherished song can instantly bring to mind the exact circumstances when it first became important, and can recreate the same sense of well-being. This may be one of the reasons why music is such a powerful tool for those working with people with dementia and Alzheimer's disease.

Our thoughts impact upon our physical body, prompting chemical changes and altering our hormonal output. Our thoughts and emotions enhance or diminish our ability to respond appropriately to danger, and affect our strength and stamina.

All of man's bodily functions are dependent on the heart.
– **The Talmud**

Experience
Hold your arm out to one side and ask a friend to
press downwards upon your wrist while you resist their
pressure. Notice the extent to which you are able to
resist, how strong you feel. Now ask them to push down

on your arm again, while asking you a question to which you reply with an untruth. Alternatively you could think about something that is not aligned to your True Nature - something that makes you feel sad, afraid or unworthy, for example. Don't worry, you don't need to stay with those thoughts for long. Has your ability to resist even the most gentle downward pressure weakened? Muscle testing, or kinesiology, offers us an opportunity to recognize the clear effect our thoughts and emotions have on our physical bodies.

The effects on the energy body and physical being are equally obvious when a third party is holding a thought or emotion about another, and even more so when a group of people are jointly cultivating a feeling about someone. Rod dowsing and muscle testing are excellent tools with which to show children how their thoughts and words can affect someone else's energy, even when they are not being intentionally unkind. Actively projecting aggressive and hurtful thoughts towards another is a basic mechanism of voodoo or black magic. Make no bones about it though, whatever you 'put out there' will sooner or later return to you. Far better, then, to notice that which is good in others, thinking thoughts and speaking words that will uplift them and generate good health and well-being for all concerned.

The better we feel, the faster our energy field vibrates, and the more rapidly synchronicities seem to occur and things come into physical manifestation. Geobiologists use the Bovis scale as a common language by which to measure the rate of vibration of people, places and things. An intensity or vibration of 6500 units on the Bovis scale is considered neutral (although this level appears to have been increasing over recent years), while the charge is considered negative and life-detracting from 0-6500 Bovis, and positive and life-enhancing once above 6500. Many expert dowsers believe that today the minimum energy level for healthy human beings is around 8000 Bovis units. I regularly use a pendulum and a simple radial Bovis meter to measure a person's rate of vibration both before and after an activity that makes them feel good, such as play, art, music, a massage, meditation or a Reiki session. People are frequently astonished to see that their Bovis reading doubles or even triples after as little as ten minutes of simple activity such as playing leapfrog, tag or hide and seek, just as we used to when we were children. Having fun and doing things that make us feel good is powerful stuff indeed! Receiving compliments from others has a similar effect.

Emotions that cause us discomfort or make us feel contracted should not necessarily be viewed as a negative thing. The further an elastic band is pulled back, the further and more rapidly it will fly forward when we let go. In a similar way, a cork held underwater will inevitably and rapidly rise to the surface as soon as the pressure is released. All serious athletes understand that contraction, resistance and acceptance of a certain degree of discomfort are all necessary for sporting progression. The Zen art of bonsai necessitates pruning, trimming and restriction in order to produce the most beautiful specimens. So too can uncomfortable emotions cause rapid expansion and spiritual growth. Rare is the competent shaman or healer who has not experienced an intensely dark night of the soul and subsequently learned how to mold their discomfort into something of great benefit and service to others. When we become very clear about what we don't want, we gain clarity about what we do want in its place. True mastery lies not in avoidance and suppressing the emotions we deem to be negative, but in not holding onto them and instead using them to gain valuable self-knowledge. Repressed emotions only build up until the resulting pressure eventually causes them to erupt violently or they express themselves as sickness. When we are able to use the insights that our emotions provide to challenge and transform our thoughts and beliefs, we are more readily able to propel ourselves to better-feeling states.

Experiencing your emotions as such is not the same as accepting them as statements of fact about your own existence.
– Seth channeled via Jane Roberts

You are only at the mercy of your emotions when you are in fear of being present with them. So many addictions stem from a resistance to feeling uncomfortable emotions, or of taking right action based upon the information they provide. Having a few drinks or smoking cannabis might have a soothing effect in the short-term, but will not resolve the underlying discord. More often than not while our addiction might temporarily dull the sensation of emotional pain, it will also take the edge off any pleasurable sensations such as joy and happiness that might also be available to us. Our failure to take responsibility or action subsequently encourages the cultivation of unhelpful feelings such as shame, guilt, worthlessness and self-pity, and thus further perpetuates the misconceptions.

Let's return to the car analogy. If emotions represent fuel for our thoughts and imagination, then gas is very helpful if we want to drive our car from A to B. However, we are no more our thoughts and emotions than the gas or the car is the person using the steering wheel, brakes and accelerator. If you are feeling overwhelmed by a certain emotion or thought, ask yourself, "Who is the thinker of this thought?" "Who is feeling this emotion?" Allow the emotion to be exactly as it is and notice how it is nothing more than a vibration, a fleeting sensation, which changes as we give it space to evolve.

Each emotion can be said to have a certain 'shape'. For example, when we are terrified or feeling particularly vulnerable we often curl ourselves up into the fetus position.

Experience

Think of something that you feel uncomfortable about, such as speaking or singing in front of a group of people. Notice how you hold yourself when you are unsure and where you direct your gaze. Do you round your shoulders and look down at your feet? Do your shoulders slump when you're feeling defeated?

We've all seen those photos of joyful women on beaches and mountaintops, arms outstretched, heads thrown back, the epitome of well-being. A simple reshaping of our physical position is a very quick way to trigger a different feeling state. Next time you are feeling unsure of yourself, simply pull your shoulders back, tilt your chin upwards and open your chest, breathing deeply into your stomach so that air moves freely throughout your body, and see how much more confident you instantly feel. Could this be where the phrase 'chin up' originates from? Research has shown that simply striking a 'power pose' for as little as a couple of minutes a day actually reprograms us to feel more empowered and creative.

Think of something sad while smiling and waving 'jazz hands'. Is the feeling of sadness mysteriously absent?

In Ayurveda, a science of medicine originating in India several thousand years ago, it is held that an individual's constitution, physical and emotional tendencies are determined at conception. The word 'Ayurveda' is a Sanskrit word meaning 'the wisdom of life', or 'the knowledge of longevity'. Each person's basic constitution or *Prakruti* is enlivened by different proportions of three main forces: Vata (Air), Pitta (Fire) and Kapha (Earth). Changes in emotional, physical, dietary and environmental conditions (weather, temperature, dryness, dampness etc.) can cause imbalances in mind, body and spirit. They can provoke temporary conditions such as weight loss or gain and irritability, and make us more susceptible to illness. As all foods have the potential to affect our emotional state, our mental clarity and our biochemistry, Eastern traditions advise the development of eating habits that are specifically supportive of our emotional well-being, and adapted to our individual constitution.

We could think of our cells as if they were 25 trillion little people, each one totally enveloped in the environment that is us. Each time we change our thoughts, emotions or diet we affect our cellular environment, for example by changing the acidity of our bodies or by flooding them with cortisol. The activity and movement of the sun, the moon, the planets and the stars impact us in a similar way, influencing us on a subtle level physically, mentally, emotionally and spiritually.

Ancient physicians and philosophers held similar views. In Hippocratic medicine the four humors of black bile, yellow bile, phlegm and blood are agents of metabolic change organized around the four elements of earth, water, air and fire. Each are associated with different temperaments, seasons, ages, bodily organs and planets. They each have specific qualities, such as cold and dry, cold and moist, hot and dry, hot and moist. They all interact with and are interdependent upon each other. The four humors theory may have originated in ancient Egypt and suggests that there are four fundamental personality types: sanguine (active, enthusiastic, sociable), choleric (fast, short-tempered, irritable), melancholic (quiet, wise, analytical) and phlegmatic (relaxed and peaceful).

And the origin of the demons which are in the whole body is determined to be four: heat, cold, wetness, and dryness. And the mother of all of them is matter.
– **The Apocryphon of John**

There are many correlations between these teachings and those shared across astrological traditions and throughout esoteric philosophy. They can also be found within the Jungian personality types and the four personality types used in Neuro-Linguistic Programming (NLP).

Traditional Chinese Medicine (TCM), which is based upon the five Taoist elements of wood, fire, earth, metal and water, or five phases, has many similarities. Each of the five elements represents an aspect of Qi life force energy, waxing and waning according to the time of day and the seasonal cycle. Emotional well-being is an extremely important aspect of TCM. Each emotion is associated with a different organ, and each organ is associated with a specific element and with certain of twelve energy pathways, known as meridians. Interior yin organs include the liver (wood), heart (fire), spleen (earth), lungs (metal), kidneys (water) and pericardium (fire), while exterior yang organs consist of the gallbladder (wood), stomach (earth), small intestine (fire), large intestine (metal), bladder (water) and triple burner (fire). The triple burner, also known as the triple warmer, is not recognized in Western medicine. The physiological function of the body depends upon harmonious relationships between yin and yang organs.

In Chinese philosophy, the fundamental, opposing principles of yin and yang are complementary and interdependent, each one unable to exist without the other. Each contains within it the seed of the other, and has the potential not only to generate change within its opposite, but to transform into it. Yin and yang can both consume and support one other. Yin is said to be feminine and characterized by principles such as darkness, solidity, passivity, the earth, the moon, negative charge, downward-seeking, wet, cold, sensitivity, intuition and emotion. Masculine yang characteristics are said to be bright, heavenly, active, the sun, positively charged, upward-seeking, dry, heat, logic, analysis and reason. Together they represent the reciprocal relationship between seen and unseen, structure and background. Taoism recognizes that the same harmonizing forces which shape nature are also responsible for the formation of our minds, and emphasizes the importance of living in harmony with one another, with the earth, and with the Universe.

Our psyche is set up in accord with the structure of the universe, and what happens in the macrocosm likewise happens in the infinitesimal and most subjective reaches of the psyche.
– **Carl Jung**

Under normal circumstances our emotions are unlikely to cause disease, unless we hold onto or repress them for long periods or if they are particularly intense, for example after a severe trauma. Feeling emotion is a perfectly natural part of being human. However, if we spend our lives struggling bitterly with our families and colleagues, or experience a prolonged period of stress or depression then the flow of qi is likely to become disrupted offering the potential for ill-health. This is a two-way process, and can create a self-perpetuating destructive cycle. Emotional disturbances can provoke imbalances in energy and blood flow which subsequently manifest in the body, just as disturbances in the organs can instigate emotional imbalances. When yang is weak a person may become tired and cold, feel sluggish and may experience digestive problems, poor circulation or lose sexual vitality. Conversely, when yin is deficient a person may, for example, feel restless and irritable, unable to relax, or suffer from insomnia. Vibrant health and well-being occur a result of the balancing of these two opposing forces.

Different emotions move energy in very specific ways and affect both the flow and direction of energy. Have you ever noticed how when someone is angry with another person they grow increasingly red in the face and their anger erupts violently outwards? They become 'hot under the collar'. Suppressing that rage, irritation and resentment, on the other hand, may cause qi to stagnate. Have you noticed how, when you are worried, your thoughts are scattered all over the place and you have difficulty concentrating? Certain emotions vibrate in a way that quite literally excites our molecules, while others have a tendency to coagulate. Sometimes, when emotional discomfort becomes overwhelming, we become so contracted that we unconsciously close down in an attempt to stop feeling. This numbed state might allow us to disassociate from the immediate highly traumatic events, but it may also prevent us from naturally discharging our emotions in a healthy way.

> I know that the hundred diseases are generated by the qi.
> When one is angry, then the qi rises.
> When one is joyous, then the qi relaxes.
> When one is sad, then the qi dissipates.
> When one is in fear, then the qi moves down.
> In the case of cold the qi collects; in case of heat, the qi flows out.
> When one is frightened, then the qi is in disorder.
> When one is exhausted, then the qi is wasted.
> When one is pensive, then the qi lumps together.
> – **The Su-Wen**

Our body communicates with us all the time, sending us messages, often in the form of discomfort or pain, to let us know when things are out of balance. Pain is like the warning light on a car dashboard. Unfortunately, instead of pulling over and topping up the oil when the light comes on, we often ignore the warning signs and drive on regardless, until the situation becomes critical. Each feeling is recorded in a different place in our body, and these locations are often deeply symbolic. The French word for illness or disease is 'maladie', or expressed another way 'la mal-a-dit'. Literally, 'the pain has spoken'.

If you judge pain, you suffer. If you listen to pain, you become free and wiser.
- **Tiger Singleton**

The information from painful memories and suppressed emotions is encoded in such a way that it interacts with the physical structure of our bodies, with our very cells. We might feel overly burdened with the weight of the world on our shoulders, we may have heartache or find ourselves in a gut-wrenching situation. Listening to the symbolism of our body talk can be a very good place to start unravelling the underlying thoughts and beliefs which are causing such discomfort. Do we feel angry because we want to be right or need to feel validated? Are we frustrated because we haven't communicated our needs clearly or do we feel misunderstood? Are we primarily focused upon what's in it for us? Perhaps our anger is inwardly directed. I once overheard a wise friend respond to a well-meaning suggestion that she 'fight' and 'battle' a cancer with the words, "Why on earth would I choose to attack myself anymore?"

The cure for the pain is in the pain.
- **Rumi**

Our body's intelligence offers us a wonderful tool for survival. "The last time I experienced this, that happened and I felt this way as a result," the body will advise. However, the drawback of this mechanism is that many situations can provoke responses which do not necessarily have any relation to, or are totally out of proportion to, the current circumstances. The body does not distinguish between a current set of circumstances and a thought about them. It responds regardless. Each thought activates a corresponding emotion, a feeling state in the body, whether we are aware of it or not. Beneath the level of awareness, the thought vibrations stimulate our ever-present cellular memory which in turn produces an emotion that corresponds to the first time that event occurred. Do you remember that feeling of utter humiliation when you were stood in front of the class and you didn't know the answer to the question the teacher was asking? Years later, you may very well feel the same sensations when someone catches you off guard in a business meeting you haven't had the opportunity to prepare for properly. We can use this principle to our advantage, by imagining situations in which we feel good so as to generate well-being.

Cellular memory can be overridden, reprogrammed, but to do so successfully requires a willingness to be inquiring and to practice diligently. For the majority of us, our usual response is to have a thought, feel the emotion that is triggered by it and then to simply react.

> *Today the mass of men are swept by the emotions and a sensitive response to circumstance; they are not swept usually by an intelligent reaction to life as it is.*
> **– Djwal Khul, 'The Tibetan', channeled via Alice Bailey**

Usually, our emotions are amplified when there is a sense of personal identification with the subject in question. 'My career', 'my family', 'my reputation', 'my property', 'my religion', 'what I believe', 'my friends', 'my country' and so on. If someone questions your personal integrity the chances are that you will feel their scrutiny far more intensely than if you were listening to a bit of gossip about someone else. If you lose your wallet your emotions will almost certainly be increased beyond the level they'd be at if you had just learned that your friend had mislaid theirs. Why is this? It's because the 'I' feels threatened in some way.

It is not enough to stop feeling an uncomfortable emotion. Ignoring it and pretending it doesn't exist will ultimately exacerbate the problem. Repressing our emotions just causes them to fester like an abscess until they burst painfully and messily to the surface. Instead we might want to ask ourselves, "What is the fear that underlies this emotion?" Every time we feel an emotion such as anger, stress, anxiety, contempt, worry, jealousy, envy or resentment you can bet your bottom dollar that there is a fear and a belief attached to it. If we look closely each time we judge another or we judge ourselves we will inevitably find a fear lurking somewhere beneath the surface. It may be tricky to identify initially, because our fears are often subtle and well-hidden and our beliefs even more so. We do not want to feel a certain way, so we bury our fears deep in our subconscious so we don't have to look at them. Many beliefs can be even harder to spot, because when we believe something that belief simply becomes 'the way things are'.

Fear constrains us. It limits our choices. It creates barriers and walls. Fear causes us to respond to life in a way that is chaotic, disordered, less efficient and unproductive. We become self-centered, confused and are far less probable to be of service to others. When we choose to courageously and consciously examine our fears then the barriers dissolve and new horizons and opportunities appear. When we are able to clearly identify our emotions it allows us to find the core belief, to root out the fear. Are you angry because someone belittled you or because there is an underlying fear that they may prevent you from having something you want to be, to do, or to have? Without fear there would be no anger. Tibetan Buddhism teaches that there are eight worldly preoccupations or concerns, 'samsaric dharmas', that govern all of our actions:

- Hope for happiness and fear of suffering
- Hope for fame and fear of insignificance
- Hope for praise and fear of blame
- Hope for gain and fear of loss.

The more that we become preoccupied with these things, the more we feel unsettled, anxious, worried, dissatisfied, and upset. We feel bitterness and resentment towards the person or organization we think is stopping us getting what we want or who we believe isn't giving us what we need. What is resentment but a spoken or unspoken expectation or disappointment? We feel jealous of those who have the things which we desire which we have yet to receive. We are furious with the person who threatens to take or damage something we consider to be ours. Even when we pray it is usually because we want something, and prayer is seldom effective if it is not heartfelt. We waste precious energy as we torment ourselves needlessly with worry about things that we have no way of changing or which may never happen.

Worry pretends to be necessary but serves no useful purpose.
– **Eckhart Tolle**

If we are worried and are able to take some action which will change the situation we are worried about then we should take action. If there is nothing we can do to change the situation then worrying is totally pointless. Worries are nothing more than mental projections, a rather peculiar form of self-torture.

I've had thousands of problems in my life. Most of which never actually happened.
– **Mark Twain**

When we are worried we are repeatedly thinking thoughts about a potential future event. We are not truly present to what is actually happening right now. Unless we are being chased by lions, or there's a fire, earthquake, tsunami or tornado, then generally speaking what is happening right now is not that threatening. And as we have seen, the more we think about something, the more likely it is to come into manifestation. Instead of accepting a situation as it is, just a reflection of our past thoughts and actions, we continue to offer vibrational resistance to the things we hope to create in its place. By worrying, we offer a vibration that is not in alignment with, and more often than not directly conflicts with, the feeling tone of those very things we so desire. We can only manifest those things we resonate with. Worrying holds us apart from things that feel good.

Worrying does not accomplish anything. Even if you worry twenty times more it will not change the situation of the world. In fact your anxiety will only make things worse.
– Thích Nhất Hạnh

Experience
If you find yourself needlessly worrying, as we all tend to do from time to time, tell yourself, "Not now. I will worry later. For the next ten minutes I will not worry." In ten minutes' time you can, of course, renew your non-worrying pledge for a further period.
The Gayatri So Hum meditation is a wonderfully simple tool which is indispensable when we are feeling worried.
Each time you breathe in allow yourself to mentally hear the sound 'So' and with each out-breath, mentally hear the sound 'Hum'. You will find that it is impossible to both worry and concentrate on the mantra and the breath at the same time. It is said to be so powerful that it is possible to be totally relaxed even while at the point of dying.

Ultimately, our endless craving for ownership, prestige, knowledge, spiritual enlightenment, recognition, security, pleasure, love and so on are just representative of our deeper desire to feel happiness. This is why non-attachment and humility are such important teachings across spiritual traditions.

O Realizer of the Transitory World. Don't have as objects of your mind the eight transitory things of the world: namely, material gain and no gain, happiness and unhappiness, things nice to hear and not nice to hear, or praise and scorn. Be indifferent.
– **Nagarjuna, Verse 29, Letter to a Friend**

External conditions are perpetually changing. Things move into our experience and then they move out again. We have an object, we lose an object, money flows in and it flows out again, just like the breath. Things decay. New things appear. Thoughts arise and then dissolve again. People evolve, and behave differently in accordance with their own personal experience. Sometimes they grow older and wiser. Sometimes their forgetting of who they are on a deeper level causes them to behave in ways which are dysfunctional, silly or downright hurtful. While we can always question our own thoughts and the behaviors that have drawn such experiences to us, we cannot control the behavior of others. We often try but it's usually futile. We haggle, we negotiate, we manipulate, we point score, we reason, we scream, we fight, we are spiteful, we seek revenge, we sulk. And, in our resistance, in our quest for control, in our not allowing someone to be as they are or something to be exactly as it is, we fuel the emotion still further. We gather further emotion-fueled thoughts about whatever it is we happen to have a bee in our bonnet about. The unpleasant situation that instigated our reaction, which may in itself have been short-lived, takes on a life of its own in our minds. We might mull on it for weeks. Our emotional responses are contagious, and provoke equally emotional reactions from other people. We allow, or even encourage, our emotions to escalate like a hurricane, disturbing situations that were previously peaceful. We may even find a perverse enjoyment in the mayhem, as they whip up all sorts of other chaos as they go and leave untold wreckage in their path. We could just step out of the path of the storm or wait for it to pass, but most of us hang on in there determinedly wanting to have our own way.

When angry count to ten before you speak. When really angry count to one hundred.
– **Thomas Jefferson**

Experience
Next time you feel an emotional situation beginning
to gain momentum, find a way that you can reflect
calmly upon the causes of your inner conflict. Don't add
further fuel to the fire. Stop trying to be right. Let go of
the need to control. Instead quietly extricate yourself
without drama and self-righteousness. Leave the room if
necessary. Go to the bathroom or step outside and take
a few deep breaths. Counting to ten may seem corny,
but it provides a delay which allows us to respond rather
than react, and distracts us from mentally fueling the
emotion still further. While we don't want to suppress
an unconstructive emotion, it's best not to pay it too
much attention either.
Once you are feeling calmer you will find it easier to
hear the quiet, inner voice of your True self. There is
no better source of emotional stability. Then you can
ask yourself, "What is the fear?" "What have I been
thinking?" "What do I believe about this situation?"

It may feel like you are backing down, but instead of merely
reacting to old cyclical triggers, you are, in fact, seeding a new
pattern from which new possibilities can grow.

In the ancient Tantric tradition there is a practice of emotional
fasting known as *Rasa Sadhana*, the Yoga of the Nine Emotions. It
recognizes nine Rasas, each of which is the essence of one of our
most fundamental emotions. Some – love, joy, wonder, courage
and peace – are desirable and to be cultivated. Others, such as

anger, sadness, fear and disgust, are frequently undesirable and unpleasant.

Each Rasa has a set of sub-Rasas and is associated with other Rasas which either support or aggravate it, or which are neutral. Each is dominated by a particular element, and holds a spiritual gift, or *Siddhi*, once mastered:

- Love (water): admiration, beauty, aesthetic sentiment, devotion – attainment
- Joy (fire): humor, laughter, satire, sarcasm – popularity
- Wonder (fire): curiosity, wonder, astonishment, mystery – lightness
- Peace (air): calmness, rest, exhaustion – anima
- Anger (fire): stress, irritability, violence – enjoyment
- Courage (water): determination, pride, confidence, concentration – power to rule
- Sadness (water): compassion, pity, sympathy – mightiness
- Fear (air): worry, nervousness, anxiety, jealousy – omnipotence
- Disgust (water): depression, dissatisfaction, vulgarity – power to assume any form.

That which we deem as being unpleasant becomes considerably more unpleasant when we allow ourselves to indulge our thoughts and emotions about it still further. When viewed like this it makes plain common sense to end our addiction to drama and stop creating ever more suffering for ourselves.

Stop! And be like the sky.
– **Mooji**

The development of emotional sobriety is highly valued in all spiritual traditions. Through practice we can dissolve the less desirable emotions without suppressing them, while cultivating those that are more desirable.

So, how can we cultivate constructive emotions while liberating ourselves from those which are destructive?

To be happy, stop being unhappy.
– Peter Marchand, from the teachings of Harish Johari

Emotional fasting
Commit to a period of time during which you temporarily choose not to engage with a specific unsupportive emotion, and instead focus fully upon one that is more agreeable. It may be for one hour, one morning, one day, one week or longer. In so doing we cultivate a better-feeling state of being. Form an intention at the beginning of the day, such as, "Today I choose not to engage with irritable thoughts. Today I am peaceful." Repeat it in your mind, say it out loud. Imagine what that might feel like, within the context of the day that lies ahead of you.

Releasing emotions with the breath
This is a very simple exercise, but extremely empowering. If you catch yourself regularly engaging with the same unhelpful emotion, take a deep breath, and consciously release the emotion on the exhale. It might help to stamp your feet as you do so. Notice yourself breathing in fresh, clean air, full of new potential. Repeat this several times.
You may want to name the emotion that feels inharmonious or uncomfortable, simultaneously saying, for example, "I am breathing out worry," either in your head or out loud. With each inhalation breathe in the opposite, saying, "I am breathing in safety" or "I am breathing in love." After a while you may find yourself

naturally wanting to shorten this to "I am loved" or "I am safe" or "loved" or "safe". As you continue you may find your words take up a natural rhythm and pattern in time with your breath. For example, "Worry out, safety in."

Like a Disney princess I sometimes find myself singing, "Let it go, let it go" as I do this, and mentally fling open imagined windows to a bright new world as I do so.

Choose happy

First thing in the morning set an intention to feel a certain way. "Today I choose to be happy," or "Today I choose to experience freedom." From the minute you get out of bed, and from now moment to now moment throughout seek opportunities to follow your joy. Navigate through your day by choosing the things that make you happiest and which create a sense of ease. Stop at regular intervals and ask, "What do I want to experience next?" Set a new intention if necessary. Become a conscious creator, aware of what you are choosing for yourself.

Make a list of nice ways to feel, states of being that you would like to experience. Write each one on a card, for example 'fun', 'peaceful', 'compassionate', 'loving', 'abundant', 'inspired', 'ease', 'contented', 'empowered', 'joyful', 'playful', 'focused'. Choose a card at random and challenge the Universe to demonstrate a multitude of ways in which you can generate that feeling, and pay attention to what happens throughout your day. Make a point of noticing every time you feel that way. Just as when you buy a new car, you suddenly seem to see the same type of car everywhere on the road, so you will begin to notice more and more of the feeling state that you have chosen to 'own'. Relish the ways in which it materializes.

Lighten up

Don't take life too seriously. Be childlike. Learn to
see the funny side when things don't work out as you
intended. Laugh at yourself, and laugh often with
others. The toughest situations feel more manageable
with a sense of humor, and laughter will quickly bring
you back into alignment.

Do your thing

Raise your vibration by doing things that you love. Sing,
dance, create, play, do some sport, challenge yourself
and step out of your comfort zone, have an adventure,
change it up a bit, try something new. When you're
'in the zone' and totally focused on something you
enjoy you will effortlessly generate more enjoyable
experiences.

Wouldn't it be nice if...

Capitalize on the power of your imagination to conjure
up things that you'd like to experience. The actor Jim
Carrey said that at the beginning of his acting career
when he was still little known he once wrote himself
a check for a large sum of money for acting services
rendered, way beyond what currently felt feasible
to him. He spent long hours dreaming of his career
successes. His reasoning was that even if his dreams
didn't materialize, he always felt much better while
he was imagining the potentials. However, he tells that
after a while of exercising his imagination in this way
he was offered an acting job in a film for which he was
paid the precise amount he had written on the check.

Each and every one of us will have unique reasons for wanting what we want. It can be fun to explore them and get to the bottom of what we truly desire. We can be certain of one thing. By focusing upon the absence of something we will create more absence of it, reinforcing the sense of lack, less than and unworthiness. The paradox is that when we are able to tune into a particular emotional frequency and achieve a certain feeling state where we are right now, regardless of the external conditions, we inevitably generate more opportunities to feel the same way. As we focus upon and celebrate each small success so we gain the momentum that will propel us towards ever greater ones.

Explore your emotional landscape

Draw four columns on a sheet of paper. Orient the page horizontally, in landscape mode. In the first column list several things that you long for. They may be things that you want to experience, things that you think will make your life better if you possess them, or a mix of the two - things you want to be, have, or do.

Now, one by one, examine your thoughts and feelings about each of the things that you desire or aspire to. In the second column write down one or two words that accurately describe how you currently feel about *not* having the first thing on your list. Take a moment to tune into how you are feeling. Notice the sensations in your body. You may find yourself becoming aware of thoughts, assumptions or situations that have contributed to these desires, or realize that they are only a subset of a deeper and more powerful belief or fear that underpins them. Do you feel contracted or expansive? Heavy or light? Where are you holding any tension? Does what you are feeling support you?

In the third column write down one or two words that sum up how you think you would feel if you possessed

the first thing you have listed in column one. What is
the feeling state that you are really trying to create?
Imagine it in intricate detail, as if it has already
happened. See it in your mind's eye, give it some
texture and context. How does it smell? Taste? What
colors do you see? What is the weather like? What do
you feel? Are you smiling? What is around you? Who is
with you? How are they responding? Tune in to your body
once again, and listen to what it has to tell you. How do
you feel now? It is common for the first words you write
down to morph as you become more familiar with what
is really going on beneath that which is shallow and
superficial. You may find that the things you originally
listed in your 'wanted' column also change.
In the fourth column list a concrete action, or actions,
that you can take in your life as it currently stands to
generate the same feeling.
Your beliefs can be modified to lift you up. Just as
we form unsupportive beliefs by repeatedly thinking
the same thoughts, so we can consciously ingrain new
beliefs by choosing and repeating kinder stories that
uplift us. Through repetition, we mentally create new
neural pathways and as we walk them again and again
we reinforce our updated beliefs.

Challenge unsupportive beliefs
If you notice a belief that is no longer in alignment
with who you now choose to be, write it down on a
card. Then firmly strike through it. As you do so make
a conscious choice to transform it into something
better-feeling. Ask for help in releasing any resistance
you have to letting go of the old way of thinking and
feeling. Ask to be made aware of anything else you may
need to understand. Now turn the card over and write

a new affirmation that better describes the new way of being you wish to integrate into your life. I call these 'flip cards' and I love to 'flip' an unsupportive way of thinking or emotion into one that is more constructive.

Use affirmations in the present tense, particularly 'I am' statements such as "I am the architect of my life," "I am open to change," "I am safe," and "I am excited by new experiences." Acknowledge the potential for the new feeling state that already exists in vibrational form. The evidence of it may not yet be obvious in the manifest world we are currently seeing before our eyes, and we may be aware of something very different vibrating within our bodies. Remind yourself that all possibilities exist. If we can imagine it, if we can *feel* it, then the potential is there. The greater portion of us, our soul, is already all of those things, and much more. You may say something along the lines of, "I am free. Today it is my intention to feel free in as many ways as possible."

Carry the card with you and look at it often throughout the day to remind yourself of the new way that you intend to feel and ensure that your new beliefs develop strong roots. You may wish to wear a bracelet or tie a piece of cotton around your wrist so that each time you look at it you are nudged to remember the new way of feeling and being that you are incorporating into your life. You will begin to accumulate a pack of 'new belief' cards, which you can return to again and again as required.

Leave key words in places that you will see often such as the screensaver on your phone or computer, stuck onto the bathroom mirror, or under a fridge magnet.

Look at the words often, explore and feel into the associated emotional state frequently, and celebrate your successes.

Sometimes, no matter how well-intentioned and open to change we are, it can be hard to decide upon the new feeling state that we want to experience with any precision. This is particularly true when we have held unhelpful, limiting beliefs for a long period of time. We have become so accustomed to feeling a certain way it can be difficult to imagine feeling any differently. In that instance remember to hand it over to the larger part of yourself, and ask to be given an intuitive nudge, so that you are shown what is best for you. You can be sure that such insight will come. It is highly unlikely, although not impossible, that we will shift from depression to joy in a matter of moments. Sometimes we must content ourselves with reaching for the next best feeling thought, and then reach again and again for a better one, until we finally end up in the feeling state which we are aiming for. Just because we choose one emotional state to experience right now does not mean that we cannot explore another tomorrow.

These practices are in no way a nonacceptance of feelings that we find disagreeable, but allow us to recognize that it is always possible to perceive a situation differently. One of the greatest causes of depression is a belief that the conscious mind is powerless when confronted with certain external circumstances that feel overwhelming. "This has happened therefore I feel this way." It is of vital importance that we recognize the existence of joyful beliefs and that we acknowledge our accomplishments.

Pleasure is fleeting and entirely dependent upon some outside circumstance, so it makes sense to seek happiness in a more durable way. A moment of pleasure may be intense and wonderful but it is likely to fade, diminishing to the point where it needs to be repeated. Too much can be cloying, or even harmful. The smell of a rose is glorious, but it would be foolish to spend all day with your nose in amongst its petals. What else of life would you be missing out on? Life is happening *right now*, it's not some future event. In longing for imagined, awaited pleasures that have not yet arrived we cause ourselves a very real sense of pain. True happiness is an inside job, and comes from having a full and grateful heart, in being of quiet service. It is absolutely possible to be happy despite adverse conditions, provided that the right attitude is cultivated. That does not mean we should shun life's pleasures, but our sense of happiness, peace and contentment should not be contingent upon them.

To the precise extent that we wallow in self-pity, what-ifs, recriminations and resentment, allowing our emotions and external circumstances to dominate our lives, do we waste the time that is available to us to live our lives fully. Instead, we *have* to get rid of our fears and insecurities and meet life on life's terms. Once we have rid ourselves of our underlying fears, then nothing anybody says or does can trigger us. We are no longer creatures of high entropy. Our entropic state is low, and that in turn gives us more clarity. We become more peaceful and contented and we are far more likely to be of service to the wider community.

Think about the things that make you happy, and the things you aspire to that you think will make you happy. How much of your happiness is derived from external circumstances, or stems from your beliefs about something to which you have attributed a label of good, bad, wanted or unwanted? Is your happiness self-generated? Are you self-supporting or is your peace-of-mind dependent upon something or someone else?

Collective Emotion

Sometimes, the emotion we are feeling does not relate to something in our individual lives, but is something that we are picking up from another or from a larger group consciousness. Horses and other herd animals, flocks of birds, shoals of fish rely on this intuitive group awareness for survival. We have forgotten how to listen to the collective consciousness of humanity, but it is no less present and available to us if we choose to tune in. Many sensitives report noticing symptoms such as a rapid heartbeat and an uncomfortable feeling in the solar plexus around the time of a major catastrophe, or an event such as a terrorist attack. This can, of course, work in a positive sense too. Have you ever attended a fabulous retreat or festival where everyone is kind, loving and full of the joy of life, and come away on a high that lasts for weeks? Have you noticed how the buzz you get from being at a really good live concert is amplified way beyond that of when you are listening to the same music with a small group of friends?

When I went to Florence in Italy, I was surprised to find myself moved to tears as I walked around the corner and saw the breathtakingly beautiful Santa Maria del Fiore cathedral for the first time. Yes, its beauty moved me, but I noticed that the sense of awe I was feeling in my heart and in my gut was considerably out of proportion to my 'actual' feelings on a personal level. It dawned on me that I must somehow have been tapping into the energies of place, into the emotion of all those millions of visitors who had rounded the same corner before me and stood gaping open-mouthed in appreciation.

Similarly, around the time I felt particularly uncomfortable about the introduction of legislation in the United States that 'I' had 'judged' to be harmful to human rights and to the planet, I noticed I was feeling a strong and uncomfortable sensation in the pit of my stomach. When I questioned the nature of the emotion I was sensing in my body I identified it as a feeling of disempowerment. Why was this? I lived in the French countryside, where these measures would have little personal impact upon me. As I remained with the emotion, an image immediately sprang to mind of a period in my teens during which I had been regularly bullied on the way home from school. Somehow a general feeling in the air on the other side of the world had triggered the memory of a time that I had felt personal powerlessness in my former home in England, and I had instinctively begun responding to it again in rural France. The vibrations resonated with something within me just as if

I were a tuning fork. Once I realized that the presence of the emotion I was sensing did not constitute a current threat to me, the sensation simply evaporated.

Perhaps this is why there is often such a huge outpouring of grief at the funerals of much-loved public figures, people that most of us have never connected with personally, or after a public tragedy. Research by the HeartMath Institute in California seems to suggest it is a possibility.

In the immediate aftermath of the 9/11 terrorist attack on the World Trade Center, within fifteen minutes of the first plane hitting the first tower, monitoring satellites detected a significant fluctuation in the earth's magnetic field. The HeartMath Institute propose that we are energetically connected, and that the cognitive functions, emotions, behavior and health of humans and animals are affected by solar, geomagnetic and other earth-related magnetic fields. After a great deal of very credible scientific research they hypothesize that the earth's magnetic field is a *"carrier of biologically relevant information that connects all living systems"*, to which the consciousness of each individual is connected, is influenced by and influences. What might be possible if larger groups of people intentionally and collectively cultivated loving and heart-centered energies? Consider how twenty minutes of stillness might contribute to a more balanced global consciousness. As we begin to better understand the relationship between the breath, air, thoughts and emotions, we must surely also start to question the potential we have collectively to contribute to and influence this field.

Empathy is the ability to sense someone else's pain, discomfort or emotion and the way they make us feel in ourselves. Compassion is a somewhat broader term involving not only an understanding of the pain of another, but a desire to somehow mitigate it. To feel with the heart of another is an ability we all have. We can often sense what is really going on under the surface of someone's superficial behavior. We can tell when someone's faking it. We intuitively know when something or someone is bad for us in some way, although we don't always listen to our instincts and get ourselves into all sorts of mischief as a result. But it takes real courage to develop these skills to the point that they become a valuable and consciously exploited tool for transformation. Empathy is like a muscle, the more we work it the stronger it gets.

Empathy is a choice, and it's a vulnerable choice. In order to connect with you, I have to connect with something in myself that knows that feeling.
– Brené Brown

Experience
If you're in any doubt as to whether you are empathic think back to the last time you were stood next to one of life's moaning Minnies. How did you feel when you were around them? Were they someone you wanted to spend time with, or were you keen to move on to something better-feeling as quickly as possible? Even when someone who is deeply miserable is silent their pain body is palpable. Unconsciously we are constantly scanning and reading the subtle energetic data emitted by those we engage with.

Being empathic is not always a comfortable experience. It asks us to sit in a space where all sensation, all emotion, all pain, is allowed to be present and to be acknowledged. It is a space in which the question 'Is this your pain or mine I'm feeling?' is ever present, even while you know that in order to be aware of that pain you must be sat in the place of no you and no I. When we are able to feel into someone else's pain, whether it be someone's aching shoulder, suppressed grief or self-loathing, what we are really feeling is its vibrational resonance with something that also exists within ourselves.

Can I sit with suffering, both yours and mine, without trying to make it go away? Can I stay present to the ache of loss or disgrace – disappointment in all its many forms – and let it open me?
– **Pema Chödrön**

Experience
Next time you notice an emotion or a sensation in your body, good questions to ask are "Where does this come from?", "How much of what I am feeling is mine?" and "Is my response proportionate to the circumstances?"

Noticing someone else's pain does not mean that we are obliged to claim it as our own. Mirroring the misery of someone who is deeply unhappy helps no one. Quite the opposite – it merely feeds their unhappiness. It is possible to be witness to the suffering of another, and to show them compassion, without suffering with them. Authentic happiness and inner peace influence the vibration of others and transform a space. They stop people in their tracks and make them ask, "What *is* that thing they've got? I want that too." Happiness lights up a room and inspires others. The happiness of just one person can radiate outwards and start a whole movement.

It is impossible to separate the mind from the heart. This is why Buddhists refer to the 'heart-mind'. Central to all is the heart, which pumps that rich, mysterious source of life, the blood, with its inherent gifts, around our bodies and which enables us to *feel* alive.

Purify your hearts, ye double-minded.
– **James 4.8**

Chapter 7

Handing It Over

The greatness of a man's power is the measure of his surrender.
– **William Booth**

The intricacies of the vibrational self are such that even after years of study we will only barely scratch the surface. The good news is that we don't need to understand these energies in order to work with them. Most of us don't have a clue what electricity is or how it works, yet we rely upon it for a multitude of tasks without hesitation. While a little insight into certain theories and processes might go some way towards soothing our logical, left-brained selves, healing and true wisdom is not the work of the objective, rational mind. The ego, of course, is heavily invested in encouraging us to believe otherwise. Finding workarounds that reassure our self-doubting, fearful inner critic is often where our greatest challenges lie.

Can you imagine being aware of all the processes taking place in the body at any one time, much less trying to control or manipulate them? The amount of information to process would be too overwhelming and at best could only be interpreted from our very linear, human perspective. Imagine, then, what processes might be going on behind all that is unseen, working at levels of which we currently have no understanding. Consider how one single act can have a knock-on effect, not only upon things in the immediate vicinity, but having an impact upon circumstances much further afield. Contemplate for a moment the organizing capability and the logistics required just to pump blood around our body or to grow a baby, let alone that required to bring a person or experience into our life.

Perhaps the single most powerful act available to a person,

no matter what situation they might be facing, is to accept that the 'small self' is not best placed to manage these monumental tasks. The more complex or overwhelming a dilemma seems to be, whether it relates directly to oneself or stems from a desire to be of assistance to another, the more this simple advice applies. Hand it over. Get out of your own way and hand it over.

Who or what we hand it over to is entirely a matter of personal choice. This is not a religious thing, although if we happen to have practices that we find supportive there is absolutely no reason to cast them aside. Choose whatever label or concept feels most appropriate. We don't even need to label. In fact it's probably better if we don't attempt to do so.

I often call it Being... it is immediately accessible to you as the feeling of your own presence.
– Eckhart Tolle

The only requirement is an acceptance that maybe – just *maybe* – there is something bigger, something grander in existence than 'small I' that might make a better job of things. There is a great river of well-being that is constantly flowing to each of us, if we would only open the sluice gates of the numerous dams we have built and let it through.

We don't need to know how the 'better job of things' might express itself or what form a solution might take. There is not even a requirement for us to believe in something great and wondrous. All that is needed is a willingness to quit playing God. It doesn't work. When perplexed, if we ask ourselves whether the 'small I' knows how best to deal with the situation we are confronted with the answer will frequently be 'no'. This is a great moment to relinquish a bit of control. When we are prepared to take a new approach and open the door of humility just a chink we will be amazed at what comes flooding through. As we *allow* ourselves to be guided by the small inner voice of spirit pouring through our heart-mind, then no matter how much outer turmoil is present in our lives, struggle somehow miraculously comes to an end and peace inevitably follows.

If this sounds like surrender to you, please don't view it as a sign of weakness. Surrender is not the same as submission. Submission is absolutely incompatible with the joyful activity of a spiritual life. Scared animals are submissive to those who dominate them. Slaves were forced into submission. Surrender is freeing. One thing that the world's most reputed spiritual teachers and healers have in common is their ability to get out of the way and to work intuitively. The greatest creative works are born from a readiness to release into the unknown. Experienced martial artists have this act of allowing down to a fine art, and practice a state of consciousness referred to by the Zen term 'Mushin', meaning 'no-mind' or 'no-ego' in the Samurai tradition. Through a combination of mindfulness, breathing techniques and 'letting go' Mushin enables them to be completely present to the moment, focused, clear-headed, calm and fearless. Bruce Lee was renowned for his ability to let these vital energies flow through him and guide him at every instant. Surrender is bad-ass courageousness. Don't let your ego tell you otherwise.

So how do we hand it over? Like everything else that is shared in this book, it is astonishingly easy. All we have to do is ask. We can do this in our head, as a purely mental process, but if we are already confused our thinking is likely to be dissipated and distracted. It can therefore be helpful to put our thoughts into words and do our asking out loud. Sound is incredibly powerful, as we have seen, although the words we use in our asking are primarily for *us*, bringing us focus and clarity of perception. The words are merely signposts. We can be as formal or as informal as we like. Ritual is certainly not prohibitive, but there is absolutely no requirement to be facing in a certain direction, to do things a set number of times or to recite prayers by rote. Prayer is merely a way of expressing an intention out loud, and intentions that are not heartfelt are rarely effective. Before too long, asking will no longer feel like making a request to some grand exterior power, but more like an intimate chat with a good friend. After all, we are chatting with an aspect of ourselves. Nevertheless, these conversations will be tinged with a sense of awe and reverence, and a feeling that we are just a tiny part of something magnificent and infinite. The more we practice the more we are filled with a sense of immense gratitude, as we begin to understand that one small act of asking can open countless doors.

Ask, and it shall be given to you. Seek, and ye shall find. Knock, and it shall be opened unto you.
– **Matthew 7.7**

Never be afraid to say, "I don't know, show me," or "What do I need to know?" The answers will come. Nobody will ever tell us we have asked too much, or have had more than our share of responses for the day. If we practice the art of surrender our Omnipresent self will inevitably steer us in the right direction and enable us to make choices which ensure that we thrive. The perceptive qualities of the brain are firmly limited to space and time. Accept that the version of you who is in this body on a planet right now is only able to understand things from a very limited perspective. Begin to trust that the eternal aspect of you has a much broader view of things. Let go of abusive self-talk and the need to plan down to the last detail and instead be open to whatever presents. Even when we surrender, most people seem to have a knack of trying to wrestle circumstances into a certain form to suit ourselves. If we're not worrying about what might happen if we don't micromanage, then we are trying to steer the outcome in a particular way. This is not true surrender, this is a form of self-control and is rooted in fear. Or we just dissolve into a puddle of overwhelm, procrastination and inaction. All we have to do is hand it over again. And again. And again. Allow yourself to become comfortable with the uncertainty of not knowing. When we have a willingness to release our fears and desires and stop trying to control everything then magic begins to happen.

... not my will, but thine, be done.
– Luke 22.42

Although we don't have to hit rock bottom before we hand things over, human nature is such that often it is only when we are faced with a catastrophe that we finally concede to let go of the reins. We may be confronted by one or a combination of personal disasters that shake us to our very core. The dark night of the soul is a precious and exciting thing. It doesn't seem to matter whether a meltdown of the egoic structure is prompted by death, divorce, debt, abuse, addiction, ill-health, a failing business venture, a change in social status, material loss, a total humiliation or some other self-destructive or self-seeking behavior. Those moments when we feel totally powerless and bereft hold hidden gold. Desperation can be the most wonderful gift, providing a turning point, just the breakthrough that is required to force us to say, "Help, I can't do this on my own." This is where transformation occurs. When the shell of the acorn disintegrates the majestic oak can begin to grow.

Even during our most heartfelt prayers our tendency is still only to request something we want. "Help me pay my bills," "Heal me," "Heal my Granny," we wail. Rather than selfishly demanding, "Give me," it is perhaps wiser that we ask to be shown what we need to know today, how we can most be of service and what our next step should be. Ask, sure in the knowing that all is well, not from an absence of wellness.

The correct prayer is therefore never a prayer of supplication, but a prayer of gratitude... an affirmation that even before you ask, I have answered.
– **Neale Donald Walsch**

We might ask for right thinking, an intuitive nudge, or for help in navigating something that overwhelms us with emotion, self-pity or resentment. Asking that is rooted in our deep compassion for the well-being of others can bring about astonishing results.

And what you call with love will come to you.
– *A Course In Miracles*

Not comfortable with the situation that we find ourselves challenged by, we ask, and ask again with increasing desperation. We remain doggedly attached to the result we wish to see, or rather, to the absence of it. We are like children on a long journey, constantly asking, "Are we nearly there yet?", even though we are well on the way to our destination. We are so busy complaining that we haven't arrived that we forget to look out of the window and enjoy the view.

Absolute surrender requires that we let go of our obsessive attachment to outcomes. It demands an acceptance that we don't necessarily have the best vantage point from which to make an informed decision. We are not always best placed to direct the drama we call life, we are merely actors in a great and vast production. We might tweak the script here and there, but we don't fully understand what is going on behind the scenes, and what changes would best enhance the overall performance.

Letting go is not the same as giving up. We can still follow our passion, trying to be the best possible version of ourselves and setting goals along the way. We can take the wheel of intention and use it to steer our life. Have dreams, by all means, but detach from needing things to look a certain way. This is the path of ease, the route to a contented and peaceful life. We will quickly find that aspiration, inspiration and the kind of energy that is firmly rooted in surrender and inner knowing are a powerful combination indeed.

Learn to seek stillness and to become quiet during moments of doubt. Those who regularly practice deliberate intention, prayer and meditation, who seek inner guidance, soon say that they would no more do without it than they would give up breathing and eating.

Of course, in order to receive we must first believe that we are worthy of receiving, and then we must allow the receiving of it. When we seek to sustain ourselves from an unlimited, infinite Source we can never fail to be nourished.

Happy is the man that findeth wisdom, and the man that getteth understanding.
For the merchandise of it is better than the merchandise of silver, and the gain thereof than fine gold.
She is more precious than rubies:
and all the things thou canst desire are not to be compared with her.
Length of days is in her right hand;
and in her left hand riches and honour.
Her ways are ways of pleasantness,
and all her paths are peace.
She is a tree of life to them that lay hold upon her:
and happy is every one that retaineth her.
– Proverbs 3.13–18

Chapter 8

The Wee Small Hours

The breeze at dawn has secrets to tell you.
Don't go back to sleep.
– **Rumi**

One of the things that continually astounded me when I first began to receive clients in my Reiki practice was how many people complained that they woke in the early hours and were unable to go back to sleep. They came looking for a solution to this interruption of their sleep pattern as a perceived problem. Was there something wrong with *all* of them?

The simple truth is that it was never intended for us to sleep seven or eight hours in one block. This is a very modern trend. In days gone by it was natural for us to go to bed much earlier, not long after darkness set in, rising early and often settling down for a nap later during the afternoon. The pace of today's modern society rarely allows for this but wise practitioners across all spiritual traditions continue to cultivate this fertile time, when we have a foot in both worlds, the physical and the spiritual.

We spend the vast majority of our waking day in a brain-wave state known as *Beta* (13–40 Hz). This is extremely important for our effective functioning as it enables us to concentrate and evaluate the data we receive through our senses. It is associated with active thought, problem solving, cognition, communication and survival. However, the Beta state is also associated with things like stress, anxiety, worry, irritability, frustration, anger and fear, all of which can contribute to disease.

Throughout the day we also dip in and out of the *Alpha* range (7.5–14 Hz), which is associated with a much more pleasurable, relaxed state such as daydreaming or light meditation. It gives us that effortless feeling that writers, artists and athletes describe as being 'in the zone', offering a gateway to our subconscious minds and encouraging stress release.

When we are sound asleep, unconscious, or in deep transcendental meditation we find ourselves swimming in *Delta* frequencies (0.1–3.9 Hz). Delta is vital for health and well-being as it is while we are in this state that our bodies have the opportunity to heal and restore themselves and to grow. It is the dominant brain-wave state of babies. Delta is the realm of the unconscious mind, where it is possible to receive information that would otherwise be unavailable. It is considered by many to be the bridge to what Carl Jung described as the "collective unconscious", the universal mind. Alcohol interferes with Delta-wave sleep, while a low carbohydrate diet encourages Delta activity and deep sleep.

Each of these brain-wave states contributes to our well-being. However, what we are interested in here is nurturing the deep richness of *'the ambrosial hours'*, when *'aha moments'* occur. It is that time when the answer to those questions you had been mentally grappling with all day and had taken to bed with you suddenly come to mind. In the early hours of the morning, when we are on the border between sleep and wakefulness, or in that brief lull just before we drop off to sleep, we are usually in a *Theta* state (4–7.9 Hz). Theta brain waves are present in the dream (REM) state, hypnosis, lucid dreaming and in deep meditation. Many people report a sense of deep spiritual connection and inner peace when in a Theta state. Interestingly, young children pass much of their normal waking day in a Theta state.

It is the childlike mind that finds the kingdom.
– Charles Fillmore

There is a natural pulse which resonates around our planet, widely known as the Schumann Resonance. It is an extremely low frequency (ELF) electromagnetic phenomenon which occurs in the cavity between the electrical, positively charged ionosphere of our planet and the negatively charged surface of the earth. It beats at a frequency of 7.83 Hz; it is surely no coincidence that this falls within the Theta range. It is noteworthy that the inside of the ionosphere is used in wireless technology to transmit information across long distances.

Theta is associated with a deeply internalized state and a quieting of the body, mind and emotions, which enables things that are normally unheard and unseen to come to awareness in the form of hypnogogic imagery. Although the Theta state can be elusive, with practice it can also be used for transforming limiting beliefs, to improve psychic abilities and intuition, and to induce states of expanded consciousness such as out-of-body experiences, remote viewing and lucid dreaming.

During the early hours while those around us are deep in slumber there is an absence of distractions and it is much easier to focus. Many of the greatest minds who have walked our planet, from scientists and inventors such as Nikola Tesla, Einstein and Edison, to inspired creatives such as Paul McCartney, James Cameron, Stephen King and Salvador Dali, are said to have produced some of their greatest work during that precious two to two-and-a-half hour period before sunrise.

In the early morning before dawn we seem to have the ability to achieve multiples of what we might have done later in the day, and we do so more quickly, effectively and with more ease. At this time the invisible, infrared rays of the arriving sunlight carry vast amounts of information. The perfect words and inspired ideas just seem to flow effortlessly onto the blank sheet of a rested mind.

This heightened stream of information is available to us all, if we are prepared to foster an early to bed, early to rise lifestyle, even if we don't always physically get out of our cozy beds to do so. Getting up early can take some discipline, although for many it occurs quite naturally. For several years now I have found that I literally get 'buzzed awake' at this time and feel much more sensitive to vibrations within the very molecules of my body, pressure changes within my inner ears and inner sounds. It is well worth it. This is a powerful time. I frequently wake with a new idea in my head, the answer to the question I have gone to sleep with or a subject to research.

The Early Bird
Aim to be in bed between 9 and 10pm each night, the earlier the better. If you are naturally a night owl, you may need to adapt your sleep pattern gently over a period of several weeks, going to bed ten or fifteen minutes earlier each week. Those extra hours before midnight are to be treasured. As the earth rotates the sun's energy moves away from you before midnight and quality of sleep is significantly enhanced. After midnight the sun's energy approaches us and is comparatively less beneficial.
If possible, avoid sleeping with your head to the north or the west so that you are in alignment with the earth's magnetic field. This will maximize internal cleansing and increase physical vitality and alertness when you awake.
Try to avoid eating anything sweet after sundown, including fruit, as this can increase brain activity and prevent us from getting a good night's rest. If you drink plenty of water during the day you are more likely to wake naturally in the early hours in order to go to the toilet.
Set a clear intention just before you drop off to sleep, for example telling yourself that you will wake up early and when you do so you will have new ideas and be deeply creative, or that the solution to a problem you

are trying to solve will become apparent to you.

Keep a pen and paper beside your bed and note any thoughts or impressions that come to mind upon waking. A modern day alternative can be to use the notes page of your mobile phone, ensuring that the backlight is not too bright, as this can throw you out of the Theta state.

On a practical note, if you are using your phone and you have a partner you prefer to stay on speaking terms with you may need to hold it under the covers while you take notes.

It can be a very helpful practice upon waking to lay still for a few minutes and try to recall what you have been dreaming about. Training ourselves to note dream content reinforces the notion that dream recall is important to us and as a result over a period of time our dreams usually become more vivid and easier to remember. Dreams contain a great deal of subtle information and symbolism that can provide invaluable insight.

Note down one or two key words that will act as triggers in the morning, rather than whole sentences, then allow yourself to fall back into the borderline sleep state, after which more ideas will occur quite naturally. Repeat the process noting down more key words, or sketching an image. Sometimes this process can continue for two or three hours and a great deal of information can be gained. Be mindful that it is very easy to fall back into deep sleep at this point, and many people find it is preferable to get out of bed, move to a different room, to a comfortable chair or sit up in bed.

You will quickly establish what works best for you. You may choose to get out of bed and use this time to enhance your meditation practice.

Arise in the midst of the night and commune with thy God. The ego will be crushed and things will be revealed to thee thou did not know before and thy path in life will be made smooth.
– **Quran**

If you are a writer, an inventor, an artist or a musician this can be the perfect time to sit down quietly and set to work. It's best to avoid strong artificial lighting, opting instead for natural light with softly moving shadow such as firelight and candlelight, as our ancestors did before us, so as to sustain and enjoy this delicious state of heightened consciousness for as long as possible.

Arise, awake, and stop not until the Goal is reached!
– **The Upanishads**

Chapter 9

Appreciation

Stay close to anything that makes you glad you are alive.
– Hafiz

Deep within each and every one of us is a small child who needs to be seen. We want so much for our efforts to be recognized and appreciated. "Did I do a good job?" "Does it please you?" "Am I on the right track?" "There is something that's really important to me that I want to share with you." We want someone to look us in the eyes when we talk, and to give us their time and full attention. We yearn – consciously or otherwise – for authentic, heartfelt engagement when we are being heard. If we are to thrive we need to feel acknowledged and valued. There are few greater pains for the infant than passing unnoticed.

Our challenge as we pass into adulthood is to understand that everybody has these needs. Instead of shouting, "Look at me, what about me?" and seeking the spotlight, it is the destiny of the spiritual adult to humbly and genuinely see the beauty in others and in all things. We cannot do this when we are sitting in judgment of someone, even though we may feel unheard by them, or they may have hurt us in some way. When we judge others we set ourselves on a pedestal, misguidedly believing that we are in some way more worthy than the one we are judging. The ego loves nothing more than to feel better than another, yet none of us can claim perfection. We are all still learning. It is impossible to be appreciative and simultaneously seething with resentment or frustration. Judgment and criticism create barriers, great dams which cut us off from the stream of well-being, whereas gratitude and appreciation increase its rate of flow, in terms of both volume and speed.

For generations we have been taught to be on high alert for that which may do us harm in order to survive. However, by focusing our attention in this way we inadvertently and very effectively reinforce the situation. If we examine our inner dialogue we will quickly come to the conclusion that we have been hypnotizing ourselves with the negative aspects that we so despise, and in doing so we increase their momentum. Remember that you, and you alone, are responsible for your thoughts, so instead of criticizing others choose to place your attention elsewhere.

Rather than further enhancing any feelings of rejection or separation try to actively practice acceptance and inclusion. Keep in mind that we're at where we're at, each of us doing the best that we can. Even if someone is behaving badly it is usually because they are hurting in some way or scared, and more often than not they will be mirroring something that also exists within us. When we find someone's behavior repulsive and repugnant, the best approach is to compassionately seek to understand the deeper issues. If nothing else, we can be glad of the clarity they provide, and of the ways in which they affirm what is unwanted so that we are better able to focus upon its alternative. Darkness is merely the absence of light, nothing more, nothing less, but without shadow and contrast there can be no form.

Seek to enhance the qualities that you value in others and develop the things that you have in common. Look for that which connects you, rather than that which divides you and nurture that. Encourage and enable, rather than restrict and control. Which schoolteacher brought the best out of you? The one who celebrated your successes, or the one who constantly told you that you were falling short and weren't good enough? Appreciate the individuality of others and the unique perspective they offer. Allow them to inspire you.

This approach should by no means be taken as a signal to ignore the things that do not allow you to live safely, nor should it facilitate the erosion of your personal boundaries. Not dwelling upon the defects of others does not mean you should not be treated with respect. If a situation occurs with which you are uncomfortable, first check in with yourself as to the reasons for this, then – if it is still appropriate – communicate your expectations clearly and calmly. Take any action that may be necessary. Once you have done so do not grumble incessantly upon perceived wrongs or use them as a tool with which to beat someone months or even years down the line.

Experience
Next time you are feeling unseen or unheard, find
as many ways as possible in which you can value and
appreciate the person who you feel was unappreciative.
Remember, to have anything you need first to give it.
Bear in mind, of course, that your belief that they were
unappreciative may not be accurate. That they may
have appreciated your efforts enormously, but – like so
many who walk upon this planet today – may simply not
have expressed their appreciation fully. Do not expect
anything in return. A moody adolescent will seldom
think beyond themselves and their immediate circle of
friends. How does it make you feel when instead of self-
seeking you respond with kindness and interest? Notice
what happens as a result.

It is a shallow life indeed if we exist merely with the intention of pleasing others and fitting in, or depriving ourselves of the joys that life has to offer. Our task, then, is the cultivation of inner satisfaction, rather than using our number of Facebook likes or latest work appraisal as a benchmark. Instead of seeking approval from an external source, the spiritual adult knows how to perceive and nurture the beauty in everything. They know to live in a perpetual sense of awe and radical appreciation.

Gratitude is a feedback mechanism to the Universe. When we radiate, "More of this please," the Universe unfailingly responds. Without passion and enthusiasm, life is dull and tasteless, but when we are grateful and enthusiastic we say yes to life. It's relatively easy to be enthusiastic for a short period of time, but keeping enthusiasm flowing steadily throughout life is an art and requires regular practice. Appreciation, whether it is for the plenitude of nature, or for the myriad of opportunities we have to connect and create, is key. Say yes and relish life. Allow life in.

If the only prayer you say in your life is thank you, it will be enough.
– Meister Eckhart

Give thanks with every word which the Creator still permits you to speak now! Then you shall also have earthly happiness, and peace will reign here on this hitherto troubled earth.
– Abd-Ru-Shin

Beauty can be found everywhere if we choose to experience it. So often we take life for granted, rather than truly appreciating it. We eat, yet we don't taste. We overlook the details: the fractals within a tree, the reflections in a puddle, a scent, a cool breeze against our skin, the beauty of an insect. We rush towards orgasm, instead of delighting in the touch of fingertips against our arm. Learn to see the miraculous in everything.

Experience
Look around you intently and notice three things that please you or arouse your curiosity in some way, things that you feel glad to have in your life, but which you had never really paid much attention to before. It may be the comfort and warmth of a blanket, the texture of a pet's fur, the timbre of someone's voice, the whirring of a fridge or the movement of leaves on a tree.

Become acutely aware of the beauty and benevolence
which surrounds you.
When we place our attention upon small things that
delight our senses and seek simple ways in which
to enhance them then we begin to live in a state of
wonder. We might increase them with a smile and by
looking deeply into the eyes of another, or by paying
a little attention to detail. Tidiness, fragrance,
decoration, sensual dance and music or art that speaks
to the soul – all add their own beauty to that which is
already beautiful. As we revel in that which surrounds
us, so we open our hearts to the world, realizing that
life is intensely beautiful and all is sacred.

Experience

Pay close attention to something that stirs you and
brings you pleasure, or allow yourself to imagine having
something that you very much desire. Immerse yourself
fully in it and notice the feelings that are stirring within
you. Where do these feelings come from? Do they come
from outside of you, from the object itself, or do they
emanate from within you? Realize that *you* generated
them, with your focused attention, and that you always
have the ability to do this. All human emotion, whether
it be love and appreciation, or revulsion and hatred,
is generated from within. Touch, see, taste, hear and
feel as fully as possible. Be totally present to the
experience. Be aware. Breathe deeply, and allow these
delicious feelings to expand throughout your body. Allow
yourself to smile inwardly, and gradually allow that
inner smile to overflow.
Next time life feels flat, dull and devoid of magic,
look around for something to appreciate or bring to
mind those things that previously aroused your senses.

Notice how you can recreate that sweetness of emotion even when the object of your desires in not physically present, simply by turning your thoughts to it. Music and scent can fast-track this process, triggering emotions that immediately take us back to the way we felt at a certain moment in time.

The one who loves everyone and everything is always in love.
— **Peter Marchand**

If you see rightly, you will see God everywhere.
— **Osho**

Heartfelt appreciation fundamentally transforms the vibration that we are offering to the universe which will always, *always*, return to us in some shape or form sooner or later. Gratitude is a state of absolute non-resistance, of allowing, a key with which to unlock the fullness of life. All states of resistance feel distinctly uncomfortable in the body, so gratitude also offers us a way in which we can feel more ease. Real gratitude, of the kind that has the ability to shift vibrational states, is not hollow or superficial. We're not talking about the little-considered thank yous we hear countless times a day from disinterested shop assistants here, or the type of sarcastic thank you that reflects disappointment or discontent. We're talking about a state of being that stirs the soul.

For what we're about to receive, may the Lord make us truly thankful.
— **Traditional Christian grace**

Gratitude is not indebtedness, which carries an assumption of repayment. It is an acknowledgement of benevolence and kindness, which enables us to connect with something greater than ourselves, be it another person or people, the magnificence of nature or a higher power. It allows us to cultivate humility and to be awed by the wonder and beauty of life, recognizing that we are just a tiny part of something infinite. It teaches us to revere and value all that exists, no matter how simple or apparently insignificant, in the knowledge that the same breath circulates throughout every manifestation of creation, visible and invisible.

A quote which is often attributed to Albert Einstein, perhaps inaccurately, is nevertheless worthy of note:

There are only two ways to live your life. One as though nothing is a miracle. The other is as though everything is a miracle.

Being thankful lifts the spirit and brings us a deep-rooted, unshakable sense of well-being. The purest expression of joy is one of genuine appreciation.

Develop the ability to express gratitude in *all* aspects of your life, even those that are unwanted, stressful and painful. Recognize the role you have played in creating them, and appreciate the lessons and growth that they bring, the contrast that they offer. This practice can help you to remain grounded even in the face of challenges, mitigating anger and worry, by shifting your mind towards abundance rather than lack. Instead of seeing ugly scars, gaze in wonder at the way your body has repaired itself and taken care of you.

A thankful person is thankful under all circumstances. A complaining soul complains even if he lives in paradise.
– **Baha'u'llah**

No matter what is presenting in your life right now, it will contain something that can be appreciated. *Always.* Even the total collapse and disintegration of something familiar creates space for something new.

Whatever you choose to do, however you choose to spend

your day, do it gratefully and do it wholeheartedly. Those who have a peaceful, grateful disposition tend to live longer, happier lives as a result.

Wisdom consists in doing the next thing you have to do, doing it with your whole heart, and finding delight in doing it.
– **Meister Eckhart**

When it comes to your day-to-day life, how do you begin your day? What energy do you bring in your interactions? How do you approach each new moment?

Experience
At the beginning and end of each day create a 'gratitude sandwich'. Before your feet touch the floor as you get out of bed, bring to mind several things for which you can be grateful or which you are looking forward to. Be glad that you have woken up to a new day and for the opportunities you have to create and connect. Notice how your day gets off to a much better start as a result. At night, reflect upon what went well during your day, lessons learned and the things that brought you pleasure. How does it affect your dream time when you do this? How do you feel on waking?
You may want to keep a gratitude diary which you can look back on in years to come, like a savings account of pleasant memories you can draw upon in difficult times. Shared gratitude journals can inspire others to notice what is good in their lives, when they might otherwise be finding it difficult to do so.
Keep a large jar and some post-it notes where they are easily accessible. Each day write down your favorite moment and pop it in the jar. At the end of the year, or if life is feeling a little bleak, tip them out and read

them, and remind yourself of all that life gives back. What do you appreciate about yourself? Do you *ever* appreciate yourself? How often? Stand in front of the mirror and examine yourself closely, without criticism. Notice the things that please you. Take a few moments to make a list of your qualities, and the things you excel at.

At times when you are finding it harder to taste the sweetness of life, set an alarm on your phone to go off every hour. When it rings look around for three things that you can find to appreciate, right now. There is no better antidote to resentment and depression than pervasive gratefulness. Value life, revere it.

Find satisfaction in what is already present, without becoming attached to it. Learn to rest in the beauty of what is, without desiring more or trying to manipulate or control. Desire just fuels resentment, jealousy and even hatred. Human nature is such that it's almost inevitable that we will have a certain level of dissatisfaction that compels us to want to improve upon something, to create afresh or to seek new experiences. We can meet our needs, but greed is never sated. The more we have the more we crave, and if we don't pay attention we can find ourselves in a never-ending cycle of craving, mentally conjuring up numerous ways in which we might be able to get our next 'fix', and wasting great quantities of vital energy in the process. More money, more luxury, more alcohol, more sex, more gadgets, more gossip, more negativity, more attention, more, more, ever more. Our addiction to more runs deep.

Be content with what you have; rejoice in the way things are. When you realize there is nothing lacking, the whole world belongs to you.
– **Lao Tzu**

Chapter 10

Integrity

The intention makes the crime.
– Aristotle

What do you demand of others that you don't do yourself? Do you, for example, want a scrupulously honest and transparent political system? Do you demand that your politicians and government are free from corruption yet fail to declare 100 percent of the cash that you earn? Maybe you have a little cleaning or lawn-mowing job, you sell your art or jewelry, or do a bit of healing work 'on the side'. Were you partially paid in cash for a business deal or a house sale? Perhaps you left that property rental off the last tax return. When was the last time you bent the truth? Did those new shoes or mountain bike really cost what you told your partner they did? Maybe you didn't tell them about your purchase at all. Have you ever withheld the truth, or manipulated it in some way so as to hold some power or gain an advantage over others? Perhaps you've embellished a resumé or fibbed about your income on a rental agreement. Such things may seem pretty innocuous, but in reality, small acts of dishonesty are a widespread and insidious rot that undermine the society in which we live.

Why do we do this? Something may have become a cultural norm and could be justified as 'just the way it is' or 'what everyone does', but look a little more closely and you will find that there is a deep-rooted fear or other emotion that underpins dishonest behavior. Perhaps you are worried that you won't have enough left over at the end of the month to care for your family after you have paid all that is due. Maybe you feel it would give your competitors the edge, or that others would have more than you. Do you want more than is reasonable? Or perhaps you are resentful at a system which you feel takes more than is appropriate, and you feel powerless to change it. Did you already know that your partner would have said no if you had asked them? Were you tiptoeing around a conversation so as to avoid a confrontation? Did you think you might lose if you had been truthful? Were you afraid someone would say you were wrong?

That which we see manifested in our personal lives and within our collective reality is only our inner reality reflected back at us.

From your Soul's perspective, of course, there is a stream of unlimited abundance that is constantly flowing to us. When we allow our integrity to be challenged in this way we cut ourselves off from that flow because of our wrong-thinking. Fear stems flow. If we are in alignment with Source, then there is an infinite range of possibilities, and countless ways in which more will be generated. Your True Self doesn't worry about how those bills can be paid or how that dress will be bought, it just knows that not only is it possible but that from the minute we had the idea it's already done. The energetic version of it already exists, all we have to do is come into alignment with the vibration of it. The Soul is excited by the unfolding of the adventure, by the deliciousness of the journey, by the discovery, by the preferences that emerge from contrast. From the Soul's perspective whatever we feed into the stream comes back multiplied, and it is a stream from which we all drink. What you and I throw into the river of life affects us all. Are we glad to contribute to a thriving society or are we reinforcing the idea of lack and corruption? Do we expect someone else to drive change, or do we come together with others and take action to transform dysfunctional, outdated and unsupportive systems? No amount of protesting will bring about lasting change if the greater majority of us do not first get honest with ourselves. While we cannot control the thoughts and behavior of others, we always have the opportunity to manage our own. When enough of us begin to do so on a regular basis, when rigorous honesty becomes the norm, so the changes will become evident in our co-created reality.

Who do you do business with? What companies do you choose to spend your money with? Have you ever examined how they invest theirs? Who is their parent company? Who are their business partners? In what ways do they contribute or exploit? Perhaps more than ever before, our ability to be informed and to decide how, where and with whom we purchase wields tremendous power to bring about radical change. How ethical are you? Do you detest intensive farming but keep buying cheap, factory-farmed meat in the supermarket or spraying pesticides on your garden because it's easier? Do you wail about the state of the planet or the mountains of plastic washed up on our beaches and consumed by marine life, yet continue to purchase goods wrapped in acres of plastic or casually toss recyclables out with other rubbish?

Are you resentful with someone – your partner, a family member, a friend or business associate – for behaving or not behaving in a certain way, yet you haven't communicated your desires clearly? Have you explained your expectations in a mature and coherent way? Have you told them how their behavior makes you feel? Expressing yourself with authenticity is crucial to any successful relationship. How genuinely do you listen? Do you look someone straight in the eye when you talk to them? Do you speak from the heart? You can spot someone insincere from a mile away. The difficult energies they are resonating with cause them to shift, twitch, or pace uncomfortably. They won't meet your gaze, but instead look away or stare at their feet. Their sentences are often poorly formulated, their voice weak. Speaking with honesty does not mean being rude or unkind. It is absolutely possible to be both truthful and compassionate.

Be honest with yourself. Regardless of what the other person has done and how hurt you may be feeling ask yourself, "How did I contribute to this situation?" "Could I have done or said anything differently?" "What can I change?" and "What can I do now to soothe things?" If you haven't been truthful in some way ask yourself, "What was the fear?" and "Is it true?" When we examine the circumstances closely we often realize that our own behavior played a big part in exacerbating them. As we start to take responsibility for our role in something we have contributed to, we can transform it more easily.

When a man points a finger at someone else, he should remember that four of his fingers are pointing to himself.
– Louis Nizer

Despite our best efforts, the person may continue to behave in a way that doesn't please us, but at least we will know that we have done everything possible to be up-front. Making decisions subsequently becomes much easier. We can choose to accept the situation as it currently stands without resentment, or we can make the necessary changes.

How true are you to yourself? How often do you do things simply because you think it's expected of you, because you don't want to hurt the feelings of another person, because 'that's how it's always done' or because you require some exterior validation of yourself? Is there something that inspires you but which you are denying yourself? How does it feel? Have the courage to own your truth and to express it fully. Learn to listen deeply and follow your heart. You have the right to feel fabulous.

Remember the lips
Where the wind-breath originated,
And let your note be clear.
Don't try to end it.
Be your note.
– Rumi

Don't die with your music still in you.
– **Wayne Dyer**

There is nothing more important than your own alignment to Source, and when we act in a way that is dishonest or unauthentic then it is *impossible* to be in alignment. This is because it is our true nature to know abundance and truth, and yet the small self, the mind, insists on spinning in the drama of some imagined future event that may cause lack or injury. Notice how lying – even the smallest of lies – feels in your body. Truth and dishonesty are two states of being that are poles apart energetically speaking, and it is this vibrational disparity between the two that feels so uncomfortable. Notice where in your body you feel it, and how contracted and heavy it feels. Begin to pay attention to what surrounds you after you have avoided being honest, and what sort of people and situations you subsequently attract.

We lie because we are afraid or are being selfish. Often something that we are afraid of feels like the hard option, but our inner guidance always seeks truth and clarity. It reveals information, it doesn't conceal it. There is little that feels more uncomfortable than our fear-based refusal to take action. If we are procrastinating about something, then it's a good sign that there is a fear lurking somewhere beneath the obvious. It is the fear that feels uncomfortable because it is not our true nature. A lack of action or transparency makes us feel out of sorts. Lying is an energy of contraction. We grow from doing the things that challenge us in some way. Oddly enough, the moment we have the courage to do or say that thing that we are so afraid of we expand beyond the old limitations that we have constructed for ourselves, and we instantly feel lighter and life responds accordingly.

Being honest with oneself requires non-judgmental self-analysis. No spiritual development is possible without first becoming aware of our flaws of character and their respective positive aspects that are currently lying dormant. Each and every character trait has a dual aspect. This ongoing process of close self-examination is never completed, and is something that we should return to again and again.

Evaluate

On one side of a piece of paper make a thorough list of what you consider to be the weak points in your character. They may include things such as:

- Self-pity
- Anger
- Resentment
- Pride
- Fear or cowardice
- Self-condemnation
- Intolerance
- Perfectionism
- Gossip
- Greed
- Dishonesty
- Impatience
- Envy
- Insincerity
- Procrastination
- Infidelity
- Not listening
- Unreliability
- Poor communication
- Closed-mindedness
- Pessimism
- Rigidity
- Worrying
- Recklessness
- Laziness
- Controlling
- Dependency
- Indecisiveness

On the opposite side of the page, make a note of the corresponding quality. So, for example, opposite 'not listening' you might decide to write 'presence' or 'compassion', and opposite 'pessimism' you may feel 'optimism' provides a good contrast.

From the list select one or two that most stand out to you as being ways in which you regularly react to the challenges of life. Write out the dual aspects of the quality in question, one on either side of a piece of paper, and carry them with you. Notice all the ways in which they manifest in your life. When you notice the shadow side of a personal quality emerging, ask yourself what drives it. Take out the piece of paper and turn to the positive aspect and ask yourself how it might be possible to employ it in the situation you are currently experiencing.

At the end of each day, ask yourself questions such as, "Where did I fail to be honest, with myself or with others?", "How could I have communicated more clearly?" or "How could I have been more transparent?"

Being honest with ourselves does not mean being hard on ourselves. Critical examination should not become an exercise in guilt and self-torture. That helps no one. Thankfully self-flagellation went out of fashion years ago. This is just a stock check, a statement of the facts as they stand at the current moment. Instead, we look with curiosity at the myriad of ways in which we might become a better version of ourselves. We can be accountable and take responsibility without judging ourselves harshly or condemning any perceived shortcomings, treating ourselves with the same kindness and compassion we would afford another. Tread gently.

There is no excellent beauty that hath not some strangeness in the proportion.
– Francis Bacon

None of us can claim to be anywhere near perfect, but if we strive to keep making the right choices we will find ourselves inching closer and closer towards the balanced, principled way of living that on some level we all yearn for.

Three things cannot be long hidden: the sun, the moon, and the truth.
– Buddha

Chapter 11

Taking Responsibility

Brethren, do not be children in your thinking. Be infants in evil,
but in your thinking be mature.
– Corinthians 14.20

We often hear talk of 'embracing the inner child', but there comes a time at which we need to evolve from our moody, teenage petulance and claim our inner adult. At some point along our journey towards spiritual adulthood we have to grow up a little and take responsibility for the role we have played in creating the situations in which we find ourselves embroiled. Instead of looking around for somebody else to blame, we begin to understand the extent to which our thoughts, words and actions have created our realities, and have inevitably drawn to us further situations of a similar nature. What we see around us is a clear reflection of where our thoughts have been. If upon looking around it feels like your ego has moved into the house next door then the only possible solution is to respond to your neighbor with tolerance, kindness and love. To do otherwise would be foolhardy in the extreme, as the laws of reciprocity are sure and thorough in their returning of like with like. In retrospect, we notice that the one common denominator in all the circumstances in which we find ourselves is that we were always present.

If we are old enough to carry car or house keys then we should also be old enough to be responsible for what we think and say. Accepting that our thoughts and reactions to apparently external triggers have contributed in some way to a current situation may feel uncomfortable, but it can be extremely liberating.

It is a painful thing to look at your own trouble and know that you

yourself and no one else has made it.
– Sophocles

When things don't work out quite as we would have hoped we have a choice. We can allow ourselves to get sucked into a downward spiral of poor-me thinking or we can take ownership and turn the situation to our advantage. Rather than paying too much attention to our toxic mind chatter, crying, "Woe is me," and "This sort of thing always happens to me," there is an alternative. We can choose to say, "Aha, here is an opportunity for me to see where I have been wrongly focused," or to ask, "What is the gift here?" or "How else might I respond?", and take the corrective action necessary to steer ourselves back on course. This is not a denial that life is sometimes painful but enables us to make peace with the circumstances.

Sometimes, if there is a considerable amount of emotional charge to a situation, even once we have decided to focus elsewhere, our thoughts about a subject may have gathered some momentum. For a while they might keep coming thick and fast, drawing attention to themselves like an unwelcome drunk at a sophisticated dinner party. Don't allow them to unsettle you and throw you off balance. Kindly acknowledge their presence, but don't encourage them to stay for the evening and keep plying them with booze. Refrain from gossiping, as that will only fuel the thoughts still further. If you don't become disheartened and stay positively focused as far as you are able, then you will soon find yourself in better company.

If only

Make a list of things in your life that you wish were different. How do the things on your list make you feel? Are you excited that they are coming? Are you enjoying the anticipation, relishing life in the meantime? Or is there a lot of 'poor me-ing' going on within your inner

dialogue? Do you feel victimized? Do you blame someone else for your current situation? Do you feel anger or resentment?
If you feel a situation is someone else's fault, could you have taken any avoidance action, or reacted differently? How did *you* contribute? How did that work out for you? Are you expecting someone else or some external event to change before you can be happy?
What about the situations you can't change? Does being resentful improve things? Or does it just make you feel worse?

Life happens. Challenges arise. People say things that would have been better left unspoken. Feelings get hurt. But, just as the screen is not the film that is projected upon it, we are not our feelings. An inherent part of human nature seems to be the compulsion to mentally relive difficult events over and over, suffering the original hurt time and time again. This abusive inner-talk is a form of self-torture, nothing more, nothing less. It unbalances us emotionally, and it frequently leads to physical illness.

Instead, acknowledge the facts as they currently stand with rigorous honesty. Associate no judgment or self-blame with the facts; it makes wonderful kindling for the emotional fires of poor-me. Look at it more along the lines of:

"I am at A and I want to get to B but I have no idea how to do that."
or
"I am at A and I have no idea where I want to get to, but I know that I don't want to be at A anymore."

You are at where you are at. You have to be clear about your current whereabouts before you can program your GPS for your next destination. Let go of abusive self-talk and move forward in the direction you wish to travel. Don't sit in your car wailing,

"I'm in London but I want to drive to Scotland." Decide upon the direction you wish to travel and start driving. Be prepared to move the steering wheel on a regular basis. You will have to make many small changes if you want to stay on the road. Know that if you take a wrong turn you can always take corrective action to steer yourself back on course.

The likelihood is that you probably won't manage this journey without a little internal messiness. However, if you persistently question the validity of your thoughts, using a gentle dose of self-deprecating humor, you will find they occupy mental space for increasingly shorter periods of time. Try and pinpoint where the fears are so that you can remove the roadblocks or navigate safely around them. This is a lifelong endeavor which becomes easier with practice, although practice is unlikely to ever make perfect. All we can do is keep showing up, time and again, with a willingness to grow and to make changes for the better.

Through discipline comes freedom.
– **Aristotle**

Freedom does not mean avoiding responsibility and breaking the rules. It involves accepting responsibility, standing on our own two feet, taking action, making our own way and finding freedom despite apparent restrictions. I used to have two dogs, one of whom was extremely biddable, the other who became totally absorbed in whatever happened to have caught his attention, oblivious to any commands from those trying to keep him safe. Guess which one spent most time off the leash?

If we're seething with anger or resentment, we need to understand what has pushed our buttons. What patterns of thinking have prompted our feelings? Most of us will automatically point the finger of blame at another person or some external circumstance. "They said or did something that made me angry." No. They may have said or done something, but how we react is down to us. Nobody 'makes' us angry. We choose to react with anger and to what extent we will nurture that anger. Our anger is our responsibility and nobody else's. It is only ever something that we feel inside ourselves. All we can do is take charge of our own broom and keep our side of the street clean. We cannot control someone else's thoughts and behavior – that's down to them – but we can take personal responsibility for our own. Our ego, of course, would have us believe that others are totally incapable of managing their own lives and that we would do a far better job. It is wiser to refuse to engage with such forceful, controlling or manipulative tactics, letting others learn their own lessons without our interference. As we develop self-mastery, so others will cease to have control over us. We manage difficult situations with inner strength, insight and understanding, not with force.

You see the sliver in your friend's eye, but you don't see the timber in your own eye. When you take the timber out of your own eye, then you will see well enough to remove the sliver from your friend's eye.
– Gospel of Thomas, Nag Hammadi Library

The pitfalls of this human tendency to sidestep taking responsibility by blaming others have been flagged up to us since the dawn of time. Today, if a God were to question why Adam and Eve had eaten the forbidden fruit, we might hear them decrying the Original sin by protesting, "Nothing to do with me, Guv."

And the man said, The woman whom thou gavest to be with me, she gave me of the tree, and I did eat.
And the LORD God said unto the woman, What is this that thou has done? And the woman said, The serpent beguiled me, and I did eat.
– Genesis 3.12–13

In truth, both were caught in the emptiness of shame and fear. When we are afraid or ashamed we have a tendency to blame anyone else but ourselves.

There was an occasion upon which I had noticed myself feeling particularly irritated by someone whose animals I had reluctantly agreed to care for. Every time they stopped by to visit I found myself becoming increasingly short with them, angry even, despite them having done absolutely nothing to instigate such a reaction. I knew it was inappropriate, but the feeling persisted regardless. When I finally allowed myself to sit quietly with my emotions and ask what they were sharing with me I quickly realized that they didn't relate to that event at all. They were but an echo of past occasions on which I'd invested a great deal of myself caring for and training other people's animals and my hard work hadn't been appropriately recognized. On more than one occasion I hadn't been paid. Indignant, I believed I'd been exploited, used, taken advantage of, disrespected. "Look at me, look at me, what about me?" an inner voice was still shouting. "Poor me, poor unseen, undervalued me." Aha, I thought, now we're getting a little closer to the heart of the issue. Self-worth and self-respect. How do I value and respect myself? What was this situation showing me? I also realized that if I had communicated my expectations clearly in the first place the issues could probably have been entirely avoided. Why had I felt uncomfortable about doing that? The disagreeable emotions I currently felt had nothing at all to do with the person in front of me, although the situation had all the potential to become a self-fulfilling prophecy if I didn't change my way of thinking. As soon as I had become conscious of my fear that I might once again be hurt or disadvantaged as a result of doing a good turn for someone, and the reasons underpinning that fear, I was able to behave more kindly. The unpleasant emotion rapidly dissipated, and I could turn my attention to the many ways that I *did* feel valued and appreciated. Once I realized how active this trigger effect was in my life I began to notice other occasions in which I was responding inappropriately to day-to-day life – to the phone call, the family visit, the knock at the door – and I could start to adapt my behavior accordingly. I was able to ask myself questions such as: "Why am I reacting like this?", "Is it still true?" and "How can I respond differently?" In several situations it also provided an ideal opportunity to demonstrate forgiveness.

Forgiveness does not mean that no harm was done. It is our refusal to hurt ourselves still further with continual thoughts and painful emotions around the subject that caused so much pain in the first place. Bitter resentment just breeds more resentment. Someone might have injured us once, but without a willingness to move on, we somehow suffer a thousand more aggressions of our own making. Instead, we can refuse to give the subject another ounce of head-space and choose to focus our attention elsewhere. Better still, we can use those very same experiences to help others through similar difficulties, thus turning our greatest challenges into something positive and life affirming. We don't stuff down our feelings, but instead we allow the pain to become our driver, our motivation for change. Forgiveness is the art of choosing acceptance over hurt, and changes things at their core. It is the ultimate act of defiance.

Of course, sometimes our inner guidance system is screaming out a loud warning that a situation is not good for us. This may not be a good person to do business with. Perhaps it's not such a great idea to launch ourselves into an intimate relationship with this particular individual right now. It is also our responsibility to take heed of that inner voice. We all have a litany of tales of how that panned out when we didn't.

For those in search of wisdom, self-searching becomes a regular habit. Self-examination requires courage and humility. We must be willing to take ownership of our beliefs and to scrutinize them if we are to grow beyond our self-imposed limitations. If they don't support us in realizing our aspirations then we must be prepared to reframe them so that they work for us, rather than clinging on to something just because we believe it. The very act of believing is itself a choice. Each and every person and every single thing in our lives is holding up a mirror that offers a reflection of our internal world, and our beliefs.

When wrong – which we humans frequently are – the spiritual adult knows the value of acknowledging their errors. Rather than simply muttering an apology that doesn't come from the heart they understand the merit of saying, *"I was wrong. Is there anything I can do to put things right?"* and then taking whatever action is necessary in order to do so.

The empowered know that their decisions – or lack of them – determine the course of their life, and take responsibility for directing it accordingly. How easy it is to ignore and deny rather than admitting and accepting, but avoidance just leaves us feeling that life is empty, oppressive or unfair. The worldly-wise intuitively know when a new course is needed, and make the necessary changes in all transparency. They no longer engineer situations so that someone else enables them to fail. They know that to blame others makes them a victim, and their willingness to take ownership creates new potentials and possibilities. Our ability to choose brings us real freedom and power, the very things we often fear. With power, of course, comes the obligation to employ it with integrity.

With great power comes great responsibility.
– **Voltaire**

You, everywhere you look
Learn to recognize yourself in others, especially those who you find the most challenging. When people and situations keep reappearing in your life with different faces, when insecurities are triggered, question what

you believe.

When unwanted, disturbing feelings threaten to overwhelm you, don't fight them or push them away. Choose them. Allow their presence without blaming someone else for the way you feel, because to do so immediately places you in the role of victim. This does not mean you want to feel that way. Remember that your feelings are generated because of the beliefs and attachments that you hold which are currently threatened. Examine them. Once you truly understand that you are just seeing yourself reflected back at you then no space remains for blame and judgment.

No matter what has happened to you in the past, the only person who can heal your wounds is you. When you have an operation, despite the helpful intervention of the surgeon, it is *your* body that repairs itself. The same is true for our mental, emotional and spiritual wounds. We may have some assistance along our route to wellness, but ultimately we are our own healers.

Let him who finds good praise Allah and let him who finds other than that blame no one but himself.
– **Hadith of Prophet Muhammad, Sahih Muslim 2577**

Our one basic responsibility is to be true to our own soul. Over time failure to be what we were created to be, to embody our uniqueness, can have a devastating effect. Everything in existence was intended to express its natural essence. Trees don't try to be anything other than tree-like. Being anything other than who we feel destined to be eats away at us, little by little. Give yourself permission to live the life you want to.

Question
Where in your life have you handed over your power?
Where are you waiting for someone to decide or make
changes for you?

We don't need permission to take responsibility for our own lives. As we mature, we become self-supporting. We don't haughtily reject others, scowling, "I can do it myself," but neither are we dependent upon others to provide us with what we think we need. We stop looking to someone else to mother or father us. We become emotionally responsible. Responsible people respect themselves, and are respected by others. So we should choose our words with care, speaking our truth without doing harm. We do our best to be kind and ethical.

We are there for others, contributing and passing on what has been learned and gained through word and deed. There's no compulsion to ram what has been learned down someone else's throat. While those new to the spiritual path might understandably want to convince as many people as possible of the benefits of what they've discovered, the wise stay comparatively silent. Instead they exude a quiet assurance, radiating a lightheartedness and an inner confidence that speaks volumes. Their inner GPS always seems to be steering them in the right direction. They have an uncanny ability to uplift others and draw out the best in people. Free from bigotry and hypocrisy, they seem tolerant of the beliefs of others and disinterested in gaining power, yet somehow opportunities to take the lead fall right into their lap. You know when they are in the room. People might not be able to define what it is they have but they cannot fail to sense it, and others, when the time is right, will naturally be drawn to it. They will become curious and want it for themselves.

As we begin to take responsibility we find that faith, a true faith, gradually becomes a working part of our lives. Faith is a living thing, and it doesn't take itself too seriously. Once we have a real understanding through personal experience then we feel lighthearted, sure of our place in Creation, safe and secure no matter what circumstances present. There is balance, not weirdness. There is no obligation to live an exclusively spiritual life, but instead spirituality becomes embodied. Real life continues, but with the logical mind as a useful tool, in its right place.

Considerate of our impact upon the world around us, we become active custodians. We accept that life does not just revolve around me, myself and I, understanding that the limits of our responsibility extend way beyond ourselves and our immediate circle of friends and family. There is no greater gift of worship than that of joyful, compassionate action.

We are made wise not by the recollection of our past, but by the responsibility for our future.
– **George Bernard Shaw**

Chapter 12

Taking Action

To give pleasure to a single heart by a single kind act is better than a thousand head-bowings in prayer.
– **Saadi**

We are often so busy waiting for conditions to be perfect that we forget that we are the creators of our lives. We wait for the right moment, for our ideal partner, more money, a better qualification, parental approval or any number of other criteria we have set for ourselves. Life is full of perfect imperfections. This is not a flaw, no mere defect. We are designed to be eternally striving for more, for better, constantly creating and evolving. Life force energy needs to keep flowing in order to remain healthy, and it perpetually seeks ways in which it can find expression. What else is boredom if not an emotional nudge to shake things up and get creative again? When energy is not free flowing it loses its vitality and we become unhealthy, in much the same way as when water stagnates or blood coagulates. Emotionally we feel 'stuck'.

The universe might be the engine that propels us forward, but if we want to reach a new destination then at some point we have to start moving towards it, continually steering and correcting our course as we go. If our aim is to see the view from the top of the mountain, then sitting at the bottom and praying will not do us much good if at some point we don't put one foot in front of the other and make our way upwards, step by step, pausing along the way to admire the magnificence of nature. We can possess all the knowledge in the world, but if we don't take action with which to put it to good use then that knowledge is worthless. It is our personal responsibility to do so.

All that is human must retrograde if it does not advance.
– Edward Gibbon

If we trace the etymology of all words relating to *knowing*, not only do they suggest acknowledgement of something greater than ourselves and the perceiving of a truth, but they give a sense of experiencing and living through. The very same words were once used to describe sexual intercourse, alluding to holy union or communion, sensual, joyful exploration together and acts of creation. The forms of thought, word and action are closely connected with each other, interwoven, with our actions being comprised of the densest gross matter. Gross matter on its own is inert and immobile, requiring spiritual energy to permeate it in order to become animated and vibrant with life. Source desires to express and understand itself through our activity; that is to say through our thoughts, words and deeds.

Wherefore by their fruits ye shall know them.
– Matthew 7.20

In order to reach a destination it is helpful to know – at least approximately – in what direction we are headed. So first we are required to decide where we are aiming. We need to envision what we want to achieve, and how we want to feel, and begin taking actions that bring us into alignment, a step or two closer. There may be a plethora of options but we make a choice, keeping the outcome in mind. Any choice. We should preferably make it from a quiet place, maybe sitting with the options for a little while and tuning into our bodies asking, "How does this choice feel?" But we make a choice. Then we put our energy fully behind whatever we have chosen, without tearing ourselves in two with 'what ifs' or regrets. We cannot make a wrong decision. Whatever we have chosen may eventually morph into something completely different, but it is only once we have made a choice that we can then begin to gather momentum and make progress. Not making a timely decision is one of the most common reasons for failure.

Make your choice. Choose to be who you want to be. Stop making excuses and telling yourself you're too old, too inexperienced, not pretty or intelligent enough, you can't afford it, it's too difficult, or that things like that don't happen to people like you. Start wherever you are at, with the tools that you have available to you. Not to do so is evading the responsibility you have towards yourself.

Choices are made today, right now, and all action is taken in this now moment. Each instant in existence is created from our decisions and reactions. Sages, magi, prophets and alchemists understand the immensity of this responsibility. They know that there is no authority beyond their own here on this earth plane, and that magic can only be worked through their choices and actions. Choose wisely and seek the opportunities for transformation. See the potential to create and then step into the space that opens for you. Respond to life and allow your soul to unfold. Do not squander life. Every moment of procrastination is an immeasurable loss. You are ready.

Begin now to be what you will be hereafter.
– Saint Jerome

We procrastinate for a variety of reasons, but upon examination they all stem from fear. Indecision, over-caution and doubt are subtle foes that often develop unnoticed into worry. There is a fine line between thorough planning and persistent stalling. If we are spending more time putting something off than it would take to actually do a task then it is time to ask ourselves why. Are we definite about our purpose, sure of ourselves and believing in what we are trying to achieve? Are we excited by the possibilities or are we afraid of what might happen? Do we anticipate poverty or failure? What sort of people have we attracted to our projects?

If we observe them they will help to clarify our own attitude. Are they enthusiastic? Do they have an abundance mind-set? Perhaps they are easily discouraged, and expecting to struggle?

Develop the habit of seeking inner counsel, and listening carefully to the advice of learned and experienced advisors, but don't pay too much heed to the opinions of others, or of jealous detractors. Remaining flexible is not the same as being easily swayed. Plan intelligently, thoroughly and with confidence, gathering the relevant facts wherever possible rather than taking a wild guess, and then act. We might be able to avoid taking action, but we won't be able to avoid the consequences of not taking action, nor can we avoid the consequences of the actions that we take.

It is not only what we do, but also what we do not do for which we are accountable.
– Molière

Be proactive. Prioritize. Make lists if you must. Edit your life regularly. What is of the most importance to you? But above all, be persistent. Persistence is the direct result of habit. Our capacity to be persistent is very much influenced by our preparedness to keep showing up, day after day, and doing something that in some way contributes to our progress, even on those occasions when we'd rather be doing something else. It requires a degree of self-discipline although it is undoubtedly easier to be persistent when we are doing something that we love. There is a clear correlation between the intensity of our passion, and our ability to sustain an effort. One of the most productive possible ways of taking action is to do something for the sheer pleasure of it. When we become absorbed in an activity because we are enjoying it, for the love of it, then our resistance dissolves and the energy that flows in enables us to feel our way to the perfect next step. Problems evaporate. Even when we are doing a task which feels like a burden, it becomes easier if we make it into a game. Having fun is one of the most powerful creative acts upon the planet, and yet we rarely give ourselves permission to do something simply because it pleases us.

Discipline teaches us to focus and avoid distractions. The cultivation of consistency helps us to act with integrity, enabling us to honor the commitments we have made. Regular practice prepares us to confront even the most daunting of challenges. Through repeated acts of courage we overcome our fears and we improve and advance. When we were learning to walk our parents didn't berate us every time we stumbled, they cheered us on. As spiritual grown-ups we have become our own cheerleaders. If we fall we pick ourselves up, dust ourselves down and we try again. We acknowledge our progress and we learn from our failures, each of which holds an equivalent advantage. We adapt and move forward.

Our avoidance of a task is often as a result of the feelings of overwhelm that accompany it. It is not necessarily the task that we are attempting to avoid, but the emotions stimulated by our own, well-rehearsed, irrational beliefs about it. So we distract ourselves with short-term mood enhancers in order to evade the emotional stimulus, only to increase its intrusiveness and intensify our inertia. If we were only to allow those feelings to be present they would soon pass, and we could choose another perspective from within our inner landscape with which to view the subject. Pain and discomfort are more often than not only temporary. Eventually they subside and are replaced by something else. A decision to quit when faced with overwhelm or temporary setback usually has much longer lasting, if not permanent, ramifications. How often we subconsciously give ourselves insurmountable challenges as a get out, so that rather than nudging forward we can throw up our hands in defeat when life becomes uncomfortable and proclaim, "It was too hard. I give in."

I will always have fears, but I need not be my fears.
– **Parker Palmer**

Our intolerance of uncertainty can keep us stuck. When we're not one hundred percent sure of how things might turn out the tendency is to avoid taking that first wobbly step, and then the next, as we gradually become sure and steady on our path. We falter with each 'I don't know', and conjure up images of all the ways that we might fall, instead of reaching up and taking the hand of a trusted guide.

Procrastination has many guises. Unsure, we overcomplicate. We imagine a task to be far greater than it really is and so we stall. Even if an endeavor seems immense it can always be broken down into smaller, more manageable segments. Or, overexcited by the choices life holds, we dither between them, becoming scattered and focusing fully on none. We take on more projects than we can realistically manage in the time available. Then, untrusting of others, we refuse to outsource, rigid and unyielding in our desire to retain control of every last little detail. Our unrelenting, anxious quest for perfection ensures we do nothing, rather than giving it our all or simply allowing ourselves to be adequate. Will we be good enough? What will others think? Will anyone even care? Will we be seen?

Perhaps, childlike, we repeatedly ask, "When is it coming? Why can't I see it yet?" lacking faith that what we have requested, although unseen, is already created, gestating and waiting for ripeness. Then, fearful that it won't arrive we ask for something else in its place, and more still. Impatient, we ask again and again, only to find that, at a moment when we are fully allowing the flow of life, they all ripen at the same time thus increasing our feelings of overwhelm. We may accelerate or diminish the speed with which we receive, but our receiving is assured.

What could possibly go right?
If you find yourself procrastinating ask yourself, "What am I afraid of?"
Now note what the best possible outcome could be and what small actions you can take to make it more likely. Is there a middle road? Can something be done in a more moderate way? Should it? Can you outsource some of the tasks? If you are unwilling to delegate examine your reasons why. Examine all perspectives. Be courageous.

Don't give up, and don't waste time vacillating. If no way exists then create one. Some things take more time than others to achieve, especially those that are valuable. The gifted martial artist, musician, horseman and gymnast all spend long years honing their skills before they arise spontaneously. Tormenting oneself by counting long months and years is a recipe for loss of heart, a formula for distraction.

Have patience. All things are difficult before they become easy.
– **Saadi**

Like the river that meets with a boulder, the master keeps advancing and evolving with ease, adapting their course if necessary but with their objective firmly in mind. By applying gradual effort, without forcing, obstacles will dissolve and the goal will eventually be attained.

Successful people tend to reach decisions quickly, and deviate from them slowly, if at all. They anticipate possible setbacks, but they don't expect them, and they develop strategies by which to overcome them. They don't petulantly burn all their bridges when the unexpected occurs, making change or retreat impossible. They remain focused and consistent in their efforts and get on with the job.

The most proficient sculptor keeps chipping fearlessly away

at the block of marble until they have produced a result that delights. The talented artist adds one brush stroke after the next, in hues and colors that they find pleasing. They sense when control and precision are called for, and when to allow the paint to mix and blend of its own accord to create something unexpected. They know when to add more texture and when to strip it back. They intuit when to take a calculated risk, and if those risks don't work out, they add another layer. They recognize when enough is enough, and when it is time to stop and let others share in the fruits of their labor.

He turns not back who is bound to a star.
– **Leonardo da Vinci**

Chapter 13

The Rhythm of Life

The movement of life has its rest in its own music.
– Rabindranath Tagore

Everything in life has a cycle and a season. Hearts beat, tides ebb and flow. Plants strive upwards for the light, reach their full splendor and then repose, cocooned, back into the dark blanket of the soil. Trees stretch their branches, brandishing tender leaves in spring just as a young girl might wear a new skirt; fresh, glorious. In quiet service, their constant give and take allows humanity to breathe. They labor to bear fruit, shared willingly with all, dazzle us with their autumn finery and then, knowing when to rest, allow their leaves to be stripped away by chill winds and to fall, decaying into sweet chaos to serve once more. The new moon gradually fills with the light of the sun and then wanes back into darkness. We have forgotten how to work in harmony with these cycles. Let nature teach you again. Learn to work with what is present. Accept what is, listen to the rhythms and dance with them. If the night feels long as you toss and turn under the magnificence of the full moon then discover what other benefits she brings, beyond sleep, and cultivate them.

As creatures of action, waiting patiently for the right moment doesn't come easily to most of us. How quick we are to judge momentum as something good, and apparent inaction as somehow being bad. There are no mistakes in this perfect Universe of ours. Every inspired musician will tell you that a carefully-timed pause in a piece of music can be as important as the notes themselves. When we dive underwater and hold our breath we can feel great anticipation as we make our way to the surface, anxious for the next gasp, for the next intake of air. A pause can build tension, heighten emotion, causing us to respond more powerfully. Alternatively it can dissipate emotions that have been building. There is no surer way to stop a heated discussion from escalating than to step back, taking a few deep breaths, and waiting before we reply or fire off that angry e-mail. Knowing when to act can make the crucial difference to the success or failure of a project.

We must learn to be still in the midst of activity and to be vibrantly alive in repose.
– **Indira Gandhi**

Instead of racing headlong ever-seeking towards the next thing that we are chasing, taking a pause enables us to appreciate life fully along the way. It gives us time to reflect so that our actions are considered and well-balanced.

Just because we can't see something happening with our eyes, don't be deceived. It does not mean that all is still beneath the surface. How much activity is going on within the acorn or the geranium in your herbaceous borders just before the new growth strives upwards through the soil in spring? In the chick before it breaks through its shell, or the caterpillar in the chrysalis? Yelling at your roses or praying for them will not make them bloom more quickly. A pause gives things time to mature, so that they are stronger and have a greater chance of survival and longevity. There is not a mother on the planet who will tell you that nine months was not worth the wait. Be patient.

Choose your moments for action wisely. Why cast your boat into the water paddling frantically against the ocean when you can wait a short while and allow the tide to take you effortlessly? Instead, learn to flow with the natural energy currents inherent in everything from the movements of the planets to the oscillating charge of an electric field.

Don't confuse patience with non-action. Spiritual energy

seeks change and movement. Even when something appears to be completely still, there is motion. Atoms, molecules, subatomic particles, quarks and leptons are constantly interacting with each other. This Universe of ours is in perpetual motion, and every motion is caused by and inspires another motion. All moving charges produce magnetic fields and rotating, twisting intrinsic angular momentum. Scientists refer to this apparent rotation of subatomic particles as 'spin'. Each spin has magnitude and direction, its own vector and geometry. This movement, this 'spin' is an essential property in the ordering of electrons and nuclei, hence it plays an important role in solid state physics and chemistry.

In physics the kinetic energy of an object is the energy it possesses due to its movement. When movement ceases, energy stops flowing. Vitality is lost and things stagnate or decay. Our bodies become unbalanced and unable to sustain the strong, healthy resonance required for physical existence. Projects falter and fail. It's OK. The Universe has a plan for that too. It's called death. Ultimately all things in the material realm disintegrate, to subsequently be recreated anew.

Phase transitions between states often involve a symmetry breaking process and are frequently accompanied by a period where things fall into chaos. Expansion and growth are not always comfortable. It is probable that we will meet with resistance as we stretch beyond our former boundaries. If we don't it's because we're moving sideways and remaining within our comfort zone, rather than making forward progress. Often we feel shaken to our core, and things become messy and uncertain as the old dissolves around us. Such change is a sign of transformation, part of the natural way of things, and is not to be feared. Many things in this transient world are beyond our control.

The healthy individual does not greedily gulp in air and then hold their breath until their lungs reach bursting point, terrified that they might run out. They breathe in and out with ease, without giving it a moment's thought whether there will be enough air for everyone. Why should it be different for anything else in the manifest world? Money flows in and it flows out, that which is stale ebbs away and fresh new things come into being.

Within the delicious sweetness of each cherry lies a less palatable stone, offering the possibility of growing a new tree capable of producing thousands more cherries. Should we fully savor the cherry, or should we throw it away because it contains something hard inside? Do we fully appreciate the potential for growth? The succulent flesh of the grape is peppered with tiny pips, yet we don't look upon them as irritations. We don't give them a second's thought. Why should we view life any differently? We can always just spit them out and enjoy the fruit. We could even create something from the pips. Grapeseed extract has numerous health benefits.

Make the best use of what is in your power, and take the rest as it naturally happens.
– **Epictetus**

All that can be perceived is one thing with two opposing sides perpetually seeking balance. If we are not creating then we are disintegrating. If something is not expanding then it is contracting. If there is no flow then there is stagnation. The rate of flow may change, and it may be punctuated by periods of stillness. The volume might increase or decrease, but life will always spin on in one direction or the other. At the center lies a void within which magic happens. It is that sacred space, that still point, a place of perfect equilibrium, which holds infinite potential for transformation, through which energy can begin to circulate in the opposite direction. It might last for only the briefest of instants but it touches all that is eternal. It takes courage to step into that void.

Don't cling stubbornly onto that which is fleeting. The old, no matter how we have outgrown it, will often feel familiar and comfortable. We might find ourselves worrying, "What if the new doesn't come?" "What form will it take?" "What flavor?" "Will we like it?" Release that which no longer serves and stride forward into the gap, trusting that the new *must* come. Nature abhors a vacuum. We can't pick up something new if we are already grasping something tightly in our hand. Let go of the lesser in order to make room for something more. Be greater. It doesn't matter what you have been. What matters is what you want to become.

While forms and perspectives change, giving us the impression that time marches unrelentingly onwards, the truth is that time, the recorder of all things, remains ever in the now moment, as does the essence of you. When you brushed your teeth this morning it was now. As you are reading this paragraph it is now. When you lay down to sleep this evening, it will be now. It is only ever now. Focus upon relishing the life you have right now in the marvelous, miraculous body that is sustaining you this very moment. Meanwhile, however, the pendulum, the metronome, of life swings on. Every action has an equal and opposite reaction, without exception, and therefore every movement in nature must be rhythmical.

Time is the measure of change.
– **Aristotle**

We have a tendency to view life in a linear fashion, but in truth all activity adopts a form which is circular, every revolution of which increases its power. Each motion forms a pattern of behavior, which is limited within a certain interval of time.

You have noticed that everything an Indian does is in a circle, and that is because the Power of the World always works in circles, and everything tries to be round... Everything the power of the world

does is done in a circle. The sky is round and I have heard that the earth is round like a ball and so are all the stars. The wind, in its greatest power, whirls. Birds make their nests in circles, for theirs is the same religion as ours. The sun comes forth and goes down again in a circle. The moon does the same and both are round. Even the seasons form a great circle in their changing and always come back again to where they were. The life of a man is a circle from childhood to childhood, and so it is in everything where power moves. Our teepees were round like the nests of birds, and these were always set in a circle, the nation's hoop, a nest of many nests, where the Great Spirit meant for us to hatch our children.
— **Black Elk**

The circumference of the circle plays a key role in the speed at which something moves. Whether we are pressing lightly upon the pedals of a bicycle until it gains momentum, or we are watching in horror as a tornado gathers its destructive power offshore, the principle is the same. If a grown adult tries ride the small-wheeled bike of a young teen they have to pedal comparatively faster in order to cover the same distance.

Speed and motion are all a matter of perspective. Without a frame of reference and an observer attached to it, they cannot be measured. The rhythm and pressure with which we push upon the pedals of the bicycle and the size of the wheel dictates at what speed the scenery around us changes. Imagine, now, that we are hurtling through empty space. How can we measure the speed at which we are traveling, if there is no other object against which to make a comparison?

Though we may never be able to comprehend human life, we know certainly that it is a movement, of whatever nature it be.
— **Nikola Tesla**

The very existence of movement implies that there is a body, a mass, that is being moved, and a force which is moving it. The Master has an awareness of what is occurring around them, but does not allow it to destabilize them. They don't flounder helplessly, overwhelmed by an effect, but instead they look inward to the cause. They are centered, balanced. They seek the calm within.

Mass has a tendency to inertia, while force tends to persist. Energy is always conserved. It can never be destroyed, it can only ever be transformed. These same general principles apply throughout the universe, in realms both seen and unseen. It is futile to fight against something that is unwanted. In our offering of resistance the laws of nature ensure that we both amplify and prolong it.

What you resist not only persists, but will grow in size.
– Carl Jung

Just as, in the physical world, a tornado gains strength in accordance with the number of revolutions that it makes, so too we aliment our thoughts and our words and empower them by repeatedly engaging with them. Instead, we would be wiser to seek to influence the transformation of an unwanted situation in some way, no matter how seemingly insignificant. We can try something different, choose another perspective or change our approach. If we offer a different vibration or rhythm we will literally sing a new song, and open up a whole new range of potentials. What is a change of frequency or vibration after all, but a change in the rhythm with which something oscillates? Brain waves are simply rhythmic, repetitive, neural oscillations. The spoken word is but an expression of vibration. Color could not exist without movement and repetition.

Every impulse that comes into being seeks to expand outwards, whether it be a desire to take action or an event which changes the momentum of an object. Sometimes this occurs faster than the speed of light, and sometimes it occurs over a period of time so long that the human mind is incapable of comprehending. We have a tendency to visualize this activity in wave patterns just as a doctor might interpret an EEG or ECG reading at the side of a hospital bed. In reality this motion is spherical and multidimensional in nature, extending outwards in all directions simultaneously. As the vibrational activity oscillates away at certain intervals, areas of high and low pressure are created; regions of compression and rarefaction in which energy or molecules are more densely or sparsely compacted, distributed in accordance with sinusoidal law.

Alternate currents, especially of high frequencies, pass with astonishing freedom through even slightly rarefied gases. The upper strata of the air are rarefied. To reach a number of miles out into space requires the overcoming of difficulties of a merely mechanical nature.
– Nikola Tesla

Life is a series of contrasts; of peaks and troughs, highs and lows, luminosity and shadow. What we are seeking invariably lies on the other side of what we fear.

Action makes the imperceptible audible. Every motion has its own sound. The sounds may differ, because they are each expressed through a different instrument, but each occurs as a result of the directing power that lies within. Sounds may harmonize with one another or they may jar and seem discordant, but the mystic knows that there is purpose to every oscillation and waveform that is set in motion by the Source of all life.

Life is a vibrant dance that can be described in a multitude of ways. The number four can be written as a word, as the symbol 4, in binary code, in terms of addition as 1+3, via multiplication as 2x2, via division as 8÷2, via subtraction as 5-1, as a fraction, in another language, as knots in a rope or as the Roman numeral IV. We can even draw a picture, but the idea remains the same.

Indeed, all these expressions are nothing more than mere concepts, different ways of expressing the same thing through the use of symbols.

While the pharmacist, physicist or mathematician might describe the rhythm of life in terms of periodicity, using algebraic formula, equations and geometry, the musician would probably express themselves very differently. Life is indeed a grand symphony, which could be envisaged as a complex orchestral score using an infinite variety of instruments. Each instrument has its own unique tone, and plays different notes at varying pitches, intervals and octaves, in combinations of whole and partial notes – breves, semi-breves, minims, crotchets and quavers. Tone and rhythm are as interdependent as time and space. Sometimes the music of life is flowing and relaxing, and at other times it is staccato or piercing and calls us to action. The great orchestral movement is one that has changes of tempo and volume, of crescendo and diminuendo. It has moments of suspense. It breathes with color and vibrancy, with life.

Each element has its own specific quality of sound. Like the gong, or the timpani drum, the sound of the earth is somewhat dull and indistinct, multilayered. It stabilizes and provides the firm foundations upon which a piece of music can be constructed or a home can be built. We can all instantly bring to mind the voice of a babbling stream or the ocean, or the sound of water being poured into a glass. It stimulates our imagination and our emotions. The human body is primarily composed of water. Impulsive fire, symbolic of rebirth, purification and transformation, crackles, whistles and roars, producing sounds which are high-pitched, such as fireworks exploding or the cacophony of war. It can make us feel snug and warm, it can stir us, alert us, or it can inspire fear and hatred. What kind of fire burns within you? Restless, playful and somewhat elusive, air rustles, wavers and whooshes and can carry the other elements with it. It announces its presence on the gentle breeze or within the violence of the storm. It can gently carry feathers and dandelion seeds or it can raze entire towns to the ground. Cleansing, invigorating, air is the bearer of our life force. It is that which knows. In astrology air is the marker of the intellectual and the abstract thinker, communicative, curious, analytical and perceptive. Air is the element of the mind, a sharer of information. The sound of ether is self-contained. Limitless, it is the undertone upon which all other sounds are based. Bearer of revelation, illumination, joy and ecstasy, it contains all color and form. Just as in a piece of music, the sound of each element can interact with the others, creating differing effects.

The sounds in silence

Cultivate silence. As you sit quietly, begin to notice the external sounds that you hear around you; the humming of the refrigerator or computer, the sound of the central heating system, the crack of ice in a glass, birdsong and the sounds of nature. Who is hearing these sounds? Now, pay attention to the sound and rhythm of your breathing, without changing it in any way. Notice how it moves inwards and outwards, connecting inner and outer worlds in sacred union. Listen to the sounds of your body. You may hear your heart beating, or the sounds of your metabolism. Notice the vibrations, or absence of them, throughout your body. Pay particular attention to any subtle changes in pressure or oscillations within your sinus cavities, full of magnetite, and inner ear, which can be particularly sensitive to magnetic fluctuations.
Close your eyes, ears and mouth to reduce external distractions and focus upon the area between your eyebrows, in the middle of your brain, known as the third eye or Ajna chakra in Sanskrit, a spiritual center via which duality is transcended. Mentally

'close' your ears and turn your attention inwards
towards the inner sounds which can only be heard with
your consciousness. Are you able to distinguish the
difference between the sounds of the illusory, material
world, and the Divine sound, that central sound of the
audible life stream?

He who hears the music of the Soul plays his part well in life.
— **Swami Sivananda**

*The melodies are a powerful magnetic force which draws the
attention inwards and makes it fully attuned to proceed up and up.*
— **Maharishi Shiv Brat Lal**

Long before we are born, our Soul has its own unique note, its
own voice. In the symphony of life, there are those who calm and
soothe, who harmonize, and there are others who bring discord and
discontent. It is human nature to seek harmony and balance. Notice
how quick we are to wince when someone sings the wrong note or
speaks a misplaced word, or when we hear the sound of nails on a
blackboard or a pneumatic drill. When we experience something
as beautiful or as uplifting, we are subconsciously acknowledging
its harmonic, rhythmic and proportionate qualities.

*I would describe, in brief, the poetry of words as the rhythmical
creation of beauty.*
— **Edgar Allan Poe**

Life cannot exist, movement cannot exist, without the presence of
rhythm. We depend upon it entirely. We breathe in and out, our
hearts beat. Modern technology now allows us to hear the sound
of living cells, each of which, when healthy, emits a specific sound
and rhythmic pattern. When cells are stressed or unhealthy they
emit a discordant, static-like noise which is distinctly unpleasant

to listen to. The relatively young science of 'sonocytology', which studies these sounds, holds great promise and may prove to be of considerable benefit in terms of medical diagnoses and treatments in the years to come. We take medicine and use alternative approaches such as acupuncture, reflexology and a change of diet to correct imbalances in flow and rhythm. Indeed, pulse diagnosis is one of the most important tools in Traditional Chinese Medicine and Ayurveda, as the quality, shape, depth, width, strength, frequency and rhythm of the pulse can give the practitioner much insight as to the nature of a pathology.

If we pay attention we can find rhythm everywhere. Birds beat their wings in order to fly. We drum our fingers on a tabletop when we are seeking inspiration. We stir a cup of tea in order to dissolve the sugar we added more rapidly. A mother soothes her crying baby by gently rocking and rhythmically patting it on the back. We divide what we perceive as time into rhythmic sections so that we can organize our day. Shamans the world over beat drums in a regular, repetitive pattern in order to provoke altered states of conscious awareness. We gather to dance ecstatically to the throb of trance music, or to raise our spirits in a nightclub. We dance to celebrate and to express ourselves. In the melodic, rhythmic practice of Kirtan chanting, the voice produces the sound, while the song is said to come from the heart. The Sanskrit notion of karma describes the rhythm of past actions.

Notice
What rhythms and patterns do you see around you? What do they teach you?

Rhythm has two distinct elements; mobility and regularity. Mobility has a forward motion and is benign, fertile, productive and progressive. It is essential to any process of creation. Regularity has a lateral movement, and actively supports, controls and sustains. When mobility and regularity clash, chaos arises, ultimately leading to decay and destruction. Hindus describe these three main principles of life as Brahma, Vishnu and Shiva – the Creator, the Sustainer and the Destroyer. It is only by acquiring an intimate understanding of the phenomenon of sound and rhythm that mankind may gain an accurate insight into the mysteries of creation. Knowledge of the creative and destructive properties of sound is key.

Among all aspects of knowledge the knowledge of sound is supreme, for all aspects of knowledge depend upon the knowing of form, except that of sound, which is beyond all form.
– Hazrat Inayat Khan

The dynamic movement-based meditation practice of 5Rhythms dancing is structured around a recognition of the ways in which people instinctively dance, often in very similar patterns. There are five phases, five patterns of movement, which are reflected over and over throughout the physical world. We see them in the journey through life from infanthood to old age, in our lovemaking, and in the breaking of a wave. Each phase is representative of one of the elements and an aspect of the psyche. Each has its own unique yet distinctive style of movement. In the ecstatic dance of life, we see a beginning, a building or crescendo, a peak, and then a coming down and an ending. In the dance, the beginning phase is fluid, flowing and circular, rounded in form with an inward movement. It is earthy, embodied and is very yin, feminine, in nature. As the dance builds it becomes more masculine and staccato. Catalyzing, it expresses itself through jerky, angular, outward movements. As the dance peaks into cathartic chaos there is a moment of letting go, of release, and of surrendering into the unexpected and unknown. The movements are uncontrolled and undisciplined like an unruly teenager, and have a downward expression. The next phase is somewhat intangible, lighter. It is uplifting, joyous, spacious, inspired and inventive, reminiscent of our Soul. The final phase, stillness, is a state of quietude, of tranquility, of peace, calm and introspection. Centered, it occurs in that formless place where mind, body and spirit are unified as one, and where boundaries melt. It is that moment at which the wave meets the hard edge of the shore and allows itself to be absorbed back into the ocean, and is typified by slow, delicate gestures, pauses and moments of torpidity.

Pay attention to the cycles of the cosmos. Become familiar with the best times to cleanse and the best times to sow or create something new. Get to know the rhythm of the moon and the planets. Notice the periods when all that is unhealthy in your life gets drawn to a head like a ripe abscess that is ready to burst and allow the process, knowing that it serves you, rather than struggling against it. Nature abhors a vacuum. The wise will be quick to choose how they fill the empty space that is subsequently created with something fresh, new and healthy.

The radiant sun, giver of life and source of all energy, impacts enormously upon our physiological and psychological well-being, and upon human consciousness. If there was no sun there would be no warmth, no life. It's that simple. The sun is the most powerful body in our sky and its 11-year cycle affects us, whether we are aware of it or not. When we are in tune with the cycles of the sun then physical health, well-being, vitality and clarity become effortless. In Surya Kriya, a potent yogic practice of great antiquity from which the 'sun salutation' originates, yogis adjust mind and body to the cycles of celestial activity so that they are in harmony with existence itself.

Solar activity, such as solar flares or coronal mass ejections, greatly affects the mental body via the central nervous system and the enteric nervous system – the 'second brain' located within the sheaths of tissue lining the stomach, esophagus, small intestine and colon – as it does all systems of electronic communication. Solar flares are also believed by many to affect the pineal gland, the pine-cone-shaped endocrine gland, so revered by seers and mystics. They may even drive the evolution of human consciousness itself.

A solar flare occurs when there is a sudden release of built-up magnetic energy, emitting radiation across virtually the entire electromagnetic spectrum, from long wavelength radio waves to high energy, short wavelength gamma rays. Such a flare (a coronal mass ejection or CME) can send a billion tons of plasma – a cloud of hot ionized gas full of positively charged ions and negatively charged electrons – hurtling into space at over a million miles per hour, with the power of 20 million nuclear bombs. Plasma, often referred to as the *'fourth state of matter'* (the others being solids, liquids and gases), responds very strongly to electromagnetic fields. Unlike gas it is capable of being held with magnetic fields, and is an excellent conductor of electricity. When this copious onslaught of electrically charged particles reaches the earth's magnetic field it frequently produces geomagnetic storms, which can be physically felt by many animals and sensitives, as well as producing observable effects near the poles, which we know as the aurora borealis or aurora australis, or Northern and Southern Lights. We can choose freely how we make use of this volatile energy.

If you have an airplane and you fly into the wind you will fly effortlessly. If you fly in the wrong direction you will crash. The wind is blowing, not to make you fly, not to make you crash. It just blows. It's up to you whether you use it to fly or to crash.
– **Sadhguru**

The moon has a profound action upon the planet, being the celestial object that is closest to our planet. As she waxes and wanes her action upon bodies of water is evident, but her influence reaches much further, affecting our circadian rhythms, our physiology and our emotional body. The moon, generating no light of her own, instead bathes in and reflects to all the light of the sun. She assists us to access that which is often buried deep within our subconscious mind, and helps us to cultivate our intuition, feelings and sensations. She nourishes us and shows us where we need to retreat in order to feel nurtured, safe and secure, just as our mother did in our uncertain youth. She encourages us to trust our instincts and feel our way through life, and teaches us when to acquiesce, to blend in, and to accept things as they are. There is much folklore around lunacy with good reason. At full moon our emotions are heightened, and the correlation between increases in admissions to psychiatric hospitals, suicides, emergency callouts and violent or irrational behavior is well-documented. All the age-old traditions take the 28-day lunar cycle into account when suggesting the most appropriate times to start new projects and to plant, to form specific intentions or spells, or to dissolve that which no longer serves or to bring something to closure. The ancient masters regularly made use of full moon meditations as a gateway to the Higher, or Divine mind, as do those practicing today.

Come on the full moon day.
– Sri Ramana Maharshi

Mystics of all traditions pay great attention to the number of times something is repeated. Repetition can have an enormous effect upon the way in which something is experienced and its intensity. Consider the soothing qualities of birdsong. A small dose of medicine may have a gentle and curative effect. Take too much and it could kill you. How often do we repeat the things we don't want, or leave the news on in the household, continually looping messages of tragedy and disaster? We learn by repeating things, finally absorbing that which is told to us again and again. We can all relate to the truth of the phrase 'practice makes perfect'.

Consider
What do you practice? Because what you practice, you will eventually get very, very good at. Do you practice the things that bring you joy? Do you practice peace? Or do you practice anger, resentment, worry and complaining?

In Freemasonry and Confucianism alike, repetition plays an important role in how philosophies are shared. For centuries, complex ceremonies and rituals involving specific numbers of people at specific times of the day or year have taken place in precisely measured buildings, formulated around precisely measured actions, accompanied by precisely measured words and music. It was said of K'ung Fu-tse: "If the mat was not straight, the Master would not sit." Correct timing is considered to be of great importance. Certain sounds seem inharmonious if they are sung at the wrong moment. Like eating a roast dinner for breakfast, wearing a dinner jacket to the pub or singing Christmas carols on the beach at the height of summer, it's untimely. It just feels wrong. Whether their practice is one of Druidry, indigenous healing ceremony, Sufi dancing, or Gregorian chanting, the Master knows that power is hidden within the mysteries of appropriate timing and repetition.

Earth, and all that exists upon her, is a reflection of the cosmos, directed by the same guiding principles that dictate the rotation of far distant planets. The more we interfere with the natural timing of things, the further we move from peace and harmony.

Allow your life to unfold naturally.
Know that it too is a vessel of perfection.
Just as you breathe in and breathe out,
there is a time for being ahead
and a time for being behind;

a time for being in motion
and a time for being at rest;
a time for being vigorous
and a time for being exhausted;
a time for being safe
and a time for being in danger.

To the sage
All of life is a movement toward perfection,
So what need has he
For the excessive, the extravagant, or the extreme?
– Lao Tzu

Chapter 14

Community

To have, give all to all.
– A Course In Miracles

Every living organism pulsates with a plethora of electrical and mechanical rhythms, influencing both physiology and behavior. When two or more independent rhythmic processes synchronize together they are said to become entrained. As one individual system interacts with another, each adjusts their oscillations until eventually they 'lock in' to something they share in common, to a common phase and periodicity. This harmonization to a single, dominant frequency is one of the reasons why dancing together to a strong rhythmic beat creates such a strong sense of bonding and community.

This natural impulse to come into sync can be seen throughout every aspect of nature. Every year, dazzling displays of fireflies flashing in unison seduce lucky spectators. Animals adjust their circadian clocks dependent upon the solar and lunar cycles, in accordance with the amount and quality of light available to them. Birds flock to the trees in their masses as night falls, and greet the dawn with glad voices. As the moon transits through her different phases she influences changes in hormonal production, and many women sync their menstrual cycles with her rhythms. Bears, bats, bees and snakes all go into hibernation. Perhaps the most astonishing of all hibernating animals is the cold-blooded tree frog of Alaska and Canada, capable of surviving some of the most dramatic temperature variations on the planet. It has developed its ability to harmonize with its surroundings to such an extent that at the beginning of winter it nestles down into the litter of the forest floor and literally freezes in sync with its environment. Ice crystals fill its abdominal cavity, envelop the internal organs and fill the layers between muscle and skin. Its liver produces copious amounts of glucose to stop the cells from freezing and bind the molecules in such a way as to prevent dehydration. Its heart stops beating, its breath stops and all movement ceases, yet it lives on in a state of suspended animation, surviving in temperatures that would be fatal to most other species. Then in spring, it rejuvenates, thawing from the inside outwards, and gaining a head start in the mating stakes, primed to create and produce anew.

Even apparently inanimate objects have a tendency to synchronize. In the 17th century the Dutch physicist and inventor of the grandfather clock noted that when he set a whole room full of pendulums in motion at different rates, after a while they would all have fallen into sync with one another. How can this be? Because, ultimately, even the most solid of objects is nothing more than an oscillation; energy vibrating in a particular way. The same universal principles apply.

The word entrainment stems from old French, and describes the way in which one element can impact upon another, dragging it along in its wake. It is associated, of course, with the word 'train' and offers a sense of manipulating something so as to achieve a desired form. Entrainment can be viewed as a form of energy ecology. It takes far less energy to work in harmony with something than it does to compete against it, and so energy is conserved. When we are in the presence of a calm and balanced person our breathing slows and we relax. We are much less likely to waste precious energy being agitated. Wild animals on the verge of charging are known to settle and walk away peacefully when confronted by stillness rather than fear and aggression. The brain waves of certain Reiki practitioners and their clients have been demonstrated to mirror each other during sessions, synchronizing in the quiet 'no-mind' yoga nidra pattern, a high voltage gamma state representative of the awakened mind. Spiritual masters such as the Dalai Lama and Amma are renowned for their ability to light up an entire room with their mere presence. We have all experienced what happens when we walk into a dark room and turn on a lamp. The light it produces is never devoured by the darkness. Instead it brings brightness, information and clarity to places that were previously obscure.

Because entrainment is such an innate process, it is of vital importance that we consciously question the value of the dominant force in any situation. We humans are great mimics, and often unconsciously imitate a person or a group that we identify with in some way. We change our accent, wear certain clothes and adopt particular beliefs in order to fit in. Sometimes we 'lose' our entire personality when we spend too long in the presence of someone who is particularly overbearing or controlling. We blend into the background, leaving truths that should have been spoken unsaid or, frustrated, we lash out in rage. What horrors await when an entire country is swept along on the tide of dictatorship?

We do not operate in isolation. Wherever we go we offer a vibration that has the potential to affect others. Do not underestimate the significance of this. It is a most powerful thing indeed.

We are one Self, a unique breath of life that lives in seven billion men and women.
– **Shakti Caterina Maggi**

So what is the dominant frequency? The most fundamental frequency is love, and it has a harmonic signature, pattern and movement that nature constantly strives to align with. It is the very basis of all existence.

Reflection
Where do you allow yourself to be dragged along by others? How might you change your behavior so that you align with the power of whole Universes, and influence others accordingly?

We cannot compel others to change. We cannot force society to change. We can only influence the hearts of others by sharing the wisdom of our own. When we begin to understand the interconnection of everything that is, then we also start to realize that nothing is totally our own. Our own bodies would be nonexistent were it not for the contribution of the entire universe in creating and sustaining them. When those things we gain are used purely for selfish reasons then our path quickly becomes beset with difficulties and disappointments. Yet greed and selfishness dissipate when we are full of generosity and our core values are anchored in a genuine desire to be of service to others. An individual may well work towards their own varied ambitions, but when they also support the whole then a mutually supportive atmosphere of trust and cooperation is generated, and life itself rushes to assist. This is synergy, a word which originates from the Greek words *'syn'* and *'ergon'*, meaning to work or take action together. Synergy is the interaction of two or more agents or forces so that their combined effect is greater than the sum of their individual parts.

Again, I say unto you, that if two of you agree on earth as touching any thing that they shall ask, it shall be done for them by my Father which is in heaven. For where two or three gather in my name, there I am in the midst of them.
– **Matthew 18.19**

Ask

Think of something you would like to have or achieve, and ask yourself, "How can I have it?" Pay attention to how you feel and the sort of thoughts that come into your mind. The likelihood is that the asking experience will feel somewhat contracted, with a tendency to be focused upon potential problem after potential problem.

Now try a different approach. We don't need to know the *how*. All will become crystal clear provided we are rightly focused. Ask yourself questions such as, "*Why* do I want to have it?", "*Who* else will benefit?" and "In what ways might others benefit?" Instead of asking, "What's in it for me?" ask, "How can this be of most service?" Rather than demanding, "What can I get?" try "What can I contribute?" Notice how much more expansive you feel in your asking, and how your focus is more solution-based. See how quickly the synchronicities line up and the opportunities put themselves on full display. When we act selflessly, for the benefit of the greater whole, we can be sure that the Universe will back us all the way.

Instead of gloomily exclaiming, "I want to be happy," try forming an intention such as, "I choose to feel more joy in my life, because when I am happy I uplift everyone around me." It has the potential to improve the lives of many more people, and is certainly more pleasant than dwelling on a perceived unhappiness. When made with sincere, heartfelt intent then such a request acts as a blessing in the truest sense of the word.

As we put this kind of asking into practice we quickly start to find that when our request is of service to others then the responses seem to flow more readily. This is not to say that we should never ask for something for ourselves, but rather that someone else should, if possible, also benefit from our asking. If you experience a healing on some level always be sure to pass it on. Whether it be by sharing your experience with someone facing a similar situation, or by actively helping, don't keep it to yourself.

> *One with true virtue always seeks a way to give.*
> *One who lacks true virtue*
> *Always seeks a way to get.*
> *To the giver comes the fullness of life;*
> *To the taker just an empty hand.*
> **– Lao Tzu**

> *There are two types of people. Those who come into a room and say,* *"Well, here I am," and those who come in and say, "Ah, there you* *are."*
> **– Frederick L. Collins**

It is often said that we have to give what we want to receive *before* we receive it, but what does this mean in practice? How can we, for example, give money if we have none to share? We have to offer the *vibration* of whatever it is that we want to create or to bring more of it into our lives. We initially do this via the gift of imagination; by repeatedly generating thoughts and emotions, and by using words that support our vision. We resonate with it. We feel and behave as if it is already there, and *then* we take action. We humans have a tendency to be concentrated entirely upon the material world. If we can't see it, touch it, taste it or smell it then we don't believe something can exist. Instead, we have to trust that the energetic version of what we are seeking is not only possible, but is already in existence in vibrational form, even though physical evidence of it may still not be tangible. If we have created it in thought, then it *must* exist. Give willingly through knowledge of the truth.

If you have ever become lucid within a dream you will

know that it is entirely possible to control the way the dream evolves to some extent, merely by directing your thoughts in a certain way, or by making precise requests. There are plentiful examples of people who have made a conscious decision to fly in their dreams, to seek inspiration for their musical and artistic creations, to experience healing, or to gain insight, clarity and wisdom about a specific subject and succeeded. It is no different in this dense, distinctly palpable reality. What sort of a future are you imagining in this existence that we are co-creating together?

Every person who has existed on the physical plane will at some point make a transition into the nonphysical, but despite appearances those who have left this earthly realm are never totally separated from those who remain in physical form. Their altered, etheric form 'overlaps' the energetic form of those still living, as do all of our energetic forms, as a group or collective consciousness. This is sometimes referred to as the Akashic record, or as morphic fields. Everyone therefore has access to all the information contained within this field in vibrational form. We just need to have asked the right question and be receptive to receive the answer. Indeed, we will never be receptive to receive an answer if we have not first asked a question. As each of us becomes interested in things throughout our lives we accumulate information about those things and add it to this field. Even when we transition back into nonphysical form, we will still know what we know and continue to be interested in those things that captivate us. Our nonphysical selves, endlessly curious, keep on gathering information, tapping into the explorations of those still in physical form in order to do so. If we want to know what has happened upon the earth, we should ask the earth. Every human event, thought, word, emotion, intention, action and experience that ever existed on earth is stored within the etheric field of our planet.

Herein lies all knowledge for you, if you would only draw it.
– **Abd-Ru-Shin**

All the great inventions of this time, which are like miracles, have come to the great minds who have, so to speak, communicated with matter, and matter has spoken with them face to face. All such great inventions are answers from the earth to the communication of these minds with matter.
– **Hazrat Inayat Khan**

Constantly available to artists, to inventors, to musicians, to writers, to scientists, to you and to me, all that data is waiting there for us whenever we need it, just as it would be in cloud computing. One gigantic Internet network of consciousness, and we have each contributed to it. Just as we might generate a search enquiry on Google, all we have to do is ask. Remember to ask, and learn how to listen. Our ancestors are still speaking with us.

We can only truly give freely when we are secure in our abilities as creators, and are fearless despite the apparent absence of something that is wanted. There will always be something new that we want, and things that we seek to change or improve. Such desires are essential for the evolutionary processes within this world of names and labels. Paradoxically, we can only really know the mysteries of the nameless when we are desireless and non-grasping.

There really is a limitless supply, ample available for everybody. We can both give and receive. Indeed, we must, for life seeks to extend in all directions. There is more than enough to go around. There is infinitely enough. One person's gain does not have to mean the lack of another. Without faith in this simple truth, our giving becomes begrudging and conditional.

When the welfare of a community becomes the central focus, rather than that of the individual, then everybody gains. Consider the human body. When 100 trillion atoms or so cooperate in harmony, exchanging their energy freely, then the cell functions perfectly. When 100 trillion cells or thereabouts do the same, then the body experiences wellness. When an individual cell or group of cells stops giving and receiving, keeping everything for themselves at the expense of other cells, then dis-ease sets in. It is a cancer. We have many names for the different expressions of it, but it all boils down to the same thing. As the disease spreads, whole sections of the bodily community – the organs, the skin, the bones, the blood – become affected, losing their ability to function, until ultimately *all* is lost. Nobody gains. It is futile to fight disease with yet more disease. The only possible solution is to restore harmony and the perfect bodily conditions, caring for each aspect of the body and its environment, providing nourishment and sustenance despite the onslaught of violent attacks. We thrive when we live within a community that shares, and we feel appreciated and loved. Our bodies, our planet are no different.

There is a magnet in your heart that will attract true friends. That magnet is unselfishness, thinking of others first... when you learn to live for others, they will live for you.
– Paramahansa Yogananda

Love. There is nothing in existence that is more important than love, and the sharing of that love with those who touch our lives. A supportive glance here, an encouraging word there, a hand held, a hug, a cheer. These are the foundations of the sort of communities that can move mountains together, built by people who care deeply and who are prepared to stand in solidarity with others when they are most in need. The generous don't conceal all they have to offer, afraid that it will be lost or stolen. Instead, they share their gifts and watch them multiply.

Fearlessness will be instilled with every small success. Once we begin to understand our place in the greater reality, and really start to pay attention to the ways in which our personal reality is constructed around our most persistent thoughts, then we gradually become more confident. Indeed, our anger at others and our desire to control or change them is often nothing more than a symptom of our insecurity in our own ability to create.

The only way to deal with an unfree world is to become so free that your very existence is an act of rebellion.
– **Albert Camus**

Reflection

Think back to the last time you gave something, and received nothing in return. Did you resent the other person? Why was this? Did you feel you had lost out? Were you expecting something, only giving conditionally? Was it something you could have created for yourself? What if the person who hadn't responded as you would have liked had a sort of spiritual blindness and could not, or would not understand these simple rules of community? Could you find compassion for them?
Have you ever resented those who appear to control the world's power and wealth? Could you hold fast to an alternative image of a world in which everybody understood their true power as creators, where nobody was afraid of being unable to pay a bill, of becoming homeless or not receiving the healthcare they needed? What would a large tax demand or red text on a bank statement matter if you *knew* beyond a shadow of a doubt that somehow - even if you didn't understand the how - the matter would be settled?

Once we shed our lack mentality and rid ourselves of fear then it doesn't matter what other people do. We might not like their actions, but they don't throw us off stride and we no longer feel the need to react angrily. We don't get stressed. Our attention is on enjoying life to the fullest because life merits our attention, our enjoyment and our appreciation. We know that the better we feel, the more juice and sweetness we get to squeeze out of life. We are mindful of what we are manifesting and feel secure in the knowledge that we can alter our course at any moment if the results are not to our liking. We seek first to understand before seeking to be understood. We become convinced that the world is fundamentally good; not in a way that blindly ignores the unpleasant, but from the sort of conviction that stems from an understanding of the truth. We take pleasure in contributing.

Nature shows us that we are weaker when we are isolated. One animal separated from the herd makes an easy target for predators. Isolation is not the same as solitude. Isolation involves pulling back from things, withdrawing, whereas solitude allows us to move towards them and to draw what we need towards us. Fear dwells in isolation, and cuts off all communication, whereas solitude allows it to flow, and for us to exist in peace. By deeply understanding the ways in which all things are interrelated, interdependent, we can magnify the strength of the individual by harnessing the power of community. We see this in acoustics: when two signals or frequencies are in phase with one another then a phenomenon is amplified.

Mass movements can be incredibly potent, often bringing transformative change. The sharing of a catastrophe will often bind a community together powerfully as they unite to jointly reach for solutions to their common difficulties. When communities synchronize and align to a shared vision the perfect conditions seem to manifest more rapidly and projects become more coherent, stable, organized and durable. The power of mutual self-advancement, the principle of 'you scratch my back and I'll scratch yours', has been a cornerstone of secret societies for countless centuries.

Entropy describes how energy is distributed and is used as a measure of the amount of disorder in a system. It gives us an indication of the extent to which something is available to contribute usefully. The concept of low entropy is more than a mere metaphor. When communities are fearful then things become unstable and more chaotic. Entropy is high, implying great uncertainty and unpredictability. When we live from the heart, with empathy, understanding and tolerance of others, then there is a high degree of coherence and consistency. We cooperate and collaborate harmoniously, we share information and communication becomes much clearer. It becomes easier to co-create and we are more productive. Entropy is low. Love is a unifying force, and society functions all the better for it.

The more we engage fully with life in our own unique way the more we contribute to the Universe's knowing of itself. Through our engagement, a thorough, embodied exploration of a myriad of available choices becomes possible. When there is sameness nothing new is born. When individuality, diversity and multiplicity combine an infinite range of new potentials becomes available. With the joining together of two apparently separate entities something different and distinct can be created.

All living organisms within an ecosystem are dependent upon genetic diversity for their survival. Too little diversity leads to inbreeding and healthy reproduction becomes fraught with difficulties. Bees fly from flower to flower, and the pollination that takes place is of benefit to many. The waste and decay of one species become the nutrients of numerous others. In Nature's delicate balancing act the removal of just one species can impact upon many others. Should the all-powerful lion, dominant predator of the African plains, fall extinct, its prey would quickly increase in population, causing available grassland to dramatically diminish. As habitats change, populations make adjustments in order to survive. Individuals develop and learn, and in so doing species adapt and co-evolve. Each small part of the whole is vital. *You* are vital. There is no one else quite like you, and the Universe needs your uniqueness.

Find your voice and inspire others to find theirs.
– Dr. Stephen R. Covey

In machine learning, co-evolutionary algorithms are used to generate artificial life and to prevent procedures from becoming stuck. Functions can have places where a maximum or minimum value is reached. On a graph this is expressed as peaks and troughs or 'hills and valleys'. While the 'top of the hill' may not be the maximum point of the whole function, locally it is. The introduction of 'co-evolving parasites' allows a new population of solutions to be generated and can considerably improve the efficiency and effectiveness of a simulated procedure.

Each system is nested within countless other systems. Every cell within an organ (itself comprised of molecules which in turn are made of atoms) coexists with other cells. Every organ exists with other organs and numerous bodily parts within a body. The body forms part of a community of other bodies and lives within a local environment, in one small corner of a planet that is teeming with life. The planet is shared with billions of other bodies. The earth herself resides within a solar system, within a galaxy – just one of billions of galaxies in our Universe. Who knows what lies beyond that?

This beautiful quote, widely although somewhat controversially accredited to Chief Seattle, sums it up perfectly:

Humankind has not woven the web of life. We are but one thread within it. Whatever we do to the web, we do to ourselves. All things are bound together. All things connect.

Experience

Deepen your relationship with Nature. Clear some space within your day in which you can be alone and silent outside, and allow yourself to become aware of your connection with all that is around you. Rather than viewing Nature as a collection of inanimate objects, of rocks, trees, grass and streams, begin to notice her vibrant living presence. Feel the wind on your face, the texture of tree bark or the soil, deeply hear the sounds she makes. So much communication takes place that we ordinarily just tune out. Lean against a tree and notice how soothed and anchored you feel. Why is this? Enjoy sitting quietly with a stone or a crystal between your two hands, and notice the subtle vibrations, heat or coolness that it emanates. Is it really inert? Explore the ways in which the different minerals have combined. Notice the myriad of things that depend upon one another for their own survival.

You may want to meditate with your eyes open, fixing your eyes upon one spot and allowing everything to come into exquisite detail. For a more active meditation macro photography, getting in really close to the smallest of objects, can be a wonderful way to appreciate the beauty of things that normally go unnoticed. Zoom right in upon a brightly colored or scented flower as a host of different insects land upon it. Pass some time idly watching the interactions within a community of ants.

Recognize that we, too, are part of Nature. What can be learned from her behavior? The earth, for example, provides solid foundations in which many different things may take root and grow strongly. Plants strive upwards for the light during phases of growth. The branches and leaves on trees become increasingly

spacious, more open, as they reach into the air in
fractal fashion. Birds stir prior to sunrise.

Collaboration, as opposed to competition, is key. Deeply question
any desire for conflict. It is always wise to challenge ourselves
before challenging others. Is the threat real or imagined? Are we
feeling judged by another, and is that feeling justified? Are we
really judging ourselves? What are we defending? Is it a valid
principle or belief? Whose belief? What other perspectives are
available to us? Those who pay close attention and walk peacefully
in harmony with entire Universes will not be impaired. The battle
will not find them.

*If a democracy is just a bunch of people advocating for their own
self-interest instead of the interest of the greater good then that's
not a democracy, that's anarchy.*
– **Abigail Disney**

Sufi Challenge
For the next 30 days:

- Do not compare
- Do not complain
- Do not criticize
- Do not condemn.

Notice the changes in your relationships with others and
in your own personal circumstances.

There are few among us who are able to say that they love
everyone unconditionally. Most of us love a select few, actively
despise others and are totally indifferent about the rest. When our
neighbor steals something from us, or we witness violence or greed
that harms others it can be hard to see beyond the personalities

and the acts themselves. As difficult as it may initially feel, it *is* possible for the evolving human to come to have love and patience for those who are at different stages of their journey. This doesn't happen overnight, it takes practice. We might not be perfect, but we can keep trudging in the direction of perfection. Little by little, instead of judging the behavior of others and being triggered by it, we begin to recognize that it is part of another's own process and evolution. It is impossible to argue with someone who is fully conscious. When there is total acceptance of someone else's unfolding, and of a situation, then there is no resistance. Clear communication becomes possible. Things only become important if we believe they are. When there is nothing to defend or attack then the energy of that which is unwanted is not amplified, and there is quickly an end to all drama.

If thou be great among men, be honored for knowledge and gentleness.
– The Emerald Tablets of Thoth

True knowledge is intangible. It is not something that can be grabbed hold of or acquired from a book. It transcends beliefs and ideas. It is something that lies within and connects us to all things, and it is when we live from the heart that we are at our most connected.

Learn to recognize the difference between judgment of others and intelligent observation and discernment. We are rarely of service to the greater whole if we are lying in a pool of blood with our arms and legs broken.

If you meet a disputant who is more powerful than you, fold your arms and bend your back.
– Kemetic saying

There are times when the astute retreat, and there are times when it is more appropriate to confront evil or to defend the vulnerable. The wild animal does not attack a pack of hounds and men with guns; instead it seeks to remove itself from danger and to go unseen. Yet how many would deem it right to stand idly by and let the violation of a child go unchallenged? To what extent would our inaction enable someone to do harm? These are extremes, the blacks and whites of life. Many are the grey areas in between.

The sage knows that that victory brings no reason for celebration. After any use of force there is a subsequent loss of power. It is better to use minimum effort to pull out a splinter in a finger than to wait for infection to set in. Seeking to reconcile rather than quarrel does not equate to being a pushover. On the contrary, it demonstrates inner strength and self-control. A heated confrontation will not make someone any more likely to agree with your point of view.

If two refuse, no one fights.
– **Joaquim Machado de Assis**

Our thoughts, words and deeds always spiral back to us sooner or later. If we hurt others, then we surely harm ourselves. If we take advantage of another, then we would be wise to prepare for the consequences that follow.

Why seeketh thou vengeance, O man! With what purpose is it that thou pursuest it? Thinkest thou to pain thine adversary by it? Know that thou thyself feelest its greatest torments.
– **Akhenaton**

The instinct for revenge may be strong, but the seeking of vengeance is the way of the narcissist and the neurotic. When we feel ridiculed, cheated or betrayed it is easy to seethe with rage. Think carefully before retaliating. Revenge is not synonymous with personal honor. It merely exacerbates circumstances that are already difficult, and where does that get us as a global community?

An eye for an eye will only make the whole world blind.
– **Mahatma Gandhi**

Stop fighting. Stop fighting others, stop fighting disease, and especially, stop fighting yourself. Don't bicker. Don't struggle. Nothing detracts from our serenity as quickly as silly squabbles over land, material goods, reputations and control. Detach from the drama and instead pay attention to the patterns of thinking that are driving it, patterns to which we are all addicted. When we fight we offer resistance, and the laws of nature ensure that wherever there is resistance things hang around for a lot longer. In physics resistance is the hindrance to the flow of a charge, a discourager of movement. The more frequently that things clash and collide, the more resistance is offered, and the longer an incident persists. It is far quicker for water in a stream to flow around a rock on the way to its destination than it is for it to persistently erode it. In life we can encourage flow by seeking mutually beneficial solutions. A win for all may initially be difficult to negotiate, but is ultimately far more constructive than one person having things all their own way. Our real strength lies in flexibility and forgiveness, in our ability to let things go and move on.

He is best of men who dislikes power.
– **Muhammad**

When we become too rigid in our expectations we start to bump into trouble. Have you noticed how the most authoritarian regimes, with all their controlling restrictions and prohibitions, are also the poorest? The greatest leaders are those that bring out the best in people, encouraging teamwork and innovation. They are master weavers, combining the skills of different individuals to achieve things that would otherwise have been impossible. They don't dominate. They allow rather than interfere, and it works. So, live and let live.

And the world will govern itself.

Therefore the sage says
I take no action and people are reformed.
I enjoy peace and people become honest.
I do nothing and people become rich.
If I keep from imposing on people,
They become themselves.
– **Lao Tzu**

We can eat healthily, we can practice breathing techniques and live a physically active lifestyle, but none of these things will contribute to longevity as significantly as living peacefully, behaving with tolerance and kindness and being of service to others. Active compassion is the foundation of vibrant good health and well-being.

Be equally grateful for what can be given, as well as for that which might be received. Our desire to acquire things and to hang onto them no matter what just sustains our sense of neediness and personal entitlement. In truth we already have everything we need at our fingertips. When we try to keep what we have received and repeatedly justify our keeping of it then difficulties inevitably follow. Those things that come to us are not for keeping, they are for giving. The most effective altruists continually look for ways in which they can use their own resources to bring about the greatest positive impact for all.

Reflection

- What can you give today?
- What can you let go of?
- What can you do for another?
- How can you make a difference?

As we discipline ourselves to find the gold in every situation we find that even the most difficult life experience holds hidden treasure. No matter how great the challenges we have faced, as we are able to overcome them, so are we able to use our personal experiences to help others to transform theirs. Even the most unwanted of experiences provides clarity as to what we want instead.

Evil as well as good, both operate to advance the Great Plan.
– **Kemetic saying**

Expressing gratitude is such a wonderfully simple way of inspiring others to become ever more altruistic and generous. When we feel appreciated, we feel great, and we will bend over backwards to reproduce that feel-good sensation again.

There is nothing, however, quite like the feeling that is generated by an act of kindness arising as an urge from the soul. When we give from the heart we are much closer to our natural way of behaving. The light, expansive, joyous feeling that results when we come into congruence with our true nature inspires us to give ever more freely. The desire to be of service is innate. It is not something that needs to be strenuously worked at, but which arises spontaneously. It is critical in the evolutionary process.

Service is not a quality or a performance.
– **Djwal Khul via Alice Bailey**

Our way of giving is far more important than what we give. Small gifts of time, attention and appreciation are precious gifts indeed. Those who give in a coldly calculating way in order to achieve material gain or to enhance their reputation will not receive the fullest of Universal blessings as their giving has not arisen from a soul impulse. True service stems from the heart, not from the scheming of the intellect. It is demonstrated with our actions. Giving does not exhaust our resources, it is simply a manifestation of the Universe reorganizing itself. Ultimately each giver, each receiver and each gift is a part of the same cosmic soup.

He gives little who gives with a frown; he gives much who gives little with a smile.
– Talmud

Giving that is rooted in the soil of the heart has no expectation of recompense. It is unconditional. It doesn't seek to get something back in return. The heart does not do someone a one-time favor and then expect a lifetime of indebtedness by way of acknowledgement. It just gives.

Experience
During the course of a day give at least three things anonymously. Give to someone who is in need, or give just for the pleasure of giving. How do you feel?

There is no wrong time to reach out and help others. If we are feeling fabulous our joy and enthusiasm for life will bubble over, uplifting and inspiring others as it does. We will demonstrate another way of thinking and being, generate options. If we are feeling down, then offering an ear to someone who needs to be heard, or helping someone else who is struggling find solutions to their challenges will provide a different perspective. Helping others feels good. Having someone around who cares feels good. When we act from the heart, the hearts of others become happy, and our heart feels lighter too. This simple change of focus away from 'poor me' brings in new energies which empower all. It's win-win. Be selfish. Help someone out.

> *Sorrow shared is halved and joy shared is doubled.*
> **– Native American saying**

Remain mindful of how the behavior of one person can impact upon the behavior of others, including our own. Behavior breeds behavior. Within a herd environment the survival instinct ensures that a stress trigger in one individual is picked up by others very quickly via a ripple effect. This sensibility is transferable across species, even when an individual is making a concerted conscious effort to control their anxiety. The highly developed intuition of the horse, whose very life prior to domestication depended upon its ability to make quick decisions and react with lightning speed, will pick up the nervousness of its rider in an instant and respond accordingly. We humans are no different, but in general we pay less attention and are somewhat slower to respond. The seasoned police officer will always advise a rookie to keep a close eye on the one or two rowdy, excitable individuals present in a crowd as they are leaving a nightclub or a football game, as trouble can escalate in moments and become difficult to contain.

> *Be a pattern to others, and all will go well.*
> **– Marcus Tullius Cicero**

How different emotional triggers manifest within a group depends largely on the extent to which those who comprise it are desensitized or have trained themselves to suppress reaction.

This energetic coherence can be used to good advantage. A coherent energy field can be both generated and enhanced by the collective intention of the members of a group. Research has shown that when there is a high degree of coherence then heart rhythms synchronize within the group, supporting the possibility of heart-to-heart bio-communication. Numerous studies have shown there is a clear correlation between synchronized group prayer and meditation, with positive social outcomes and health benefits for the individuals concerned. When a group of people are simultaneously experiencing feelings of inner peace, their harmonious state radiates in such a way that it can have an influence upon others much further afield. If the consciousness of one person alone has the potential to influence physical reality, as science is beginning to show is the case, then the focused intentions of a larger group are potent indeed. When those participating first clear their minds, then enter a meditative state holding a clear, shared intention, the group consciousness shifts from mere wishful thinking to actively influencing that unseen field through which life pours. Heartfelt asking and a genuine desire for transformation of some kind shared by a small collective can be incredibly transformative, as groups of healers all around the world, women gathering in circle and people joining in prayer will readily attest. We can make any agreement we choose to with the Universe. When we make it with others, on behalf of others, the Universe will rush to support us.

In union there is strength!
– Napoleon Hill

Such circles are increasingly becoming not only a place for ritual, but part of our daily lives. Non-hierarchical, sometimes virtual, yet always powerful. Points of connection at which people join together with a common focus, supporting one another, sharing their knowledge, ideas and wisdom, concentrating and magnifying their intention in ways that are of service to others. We all long for a deeper connection but women in particular seem called to sit in this way. The sacred practice of women coming together to share their wisdom, compassion and love, and to share their heartfelt teachings with their communities once formed an integral part of ancient cultures the world over. Today, people of all cultures and backgrounds are coming together in a different, more modern but no less valuable way. They are joining together all around the world, in online healing, meditation and satsang. There are groups for crafters and writers, mother and toddler support groups, virtual places where out-of-body explorers and lucid dreamers can meet to share their experiences, groups for the sharing of channeled teachings and esoteric readings. Yes, there are also places where extremists meet, porn is shared and we can learn how to make homemade explosives, but free choice, as always, remains paramount.

What possibilities might such groups hold? For centuries societies have gathered in secret to use these basic natural laws to enhance one another's wealth and power. What potentials exist when people instead gather with the intention of finding solutions to issues such as family or neighbor disputes, addiction, homelessness, poverty, pollution, education or economic challenges? Inspired solutions that work for all, and that are in harmony with the natural flow of life. Harnessing the inherent power of unity consciousness to provide inspiration for art, music and literature, or for innovative new technologies, new ways of learning, of improved societal structures? This is our birth right. This is possible right now.

Manifest the divinity that is within you, and everything will be harmoniously arranged around it.
– **Swami Vivekananda**

Such things begin in small ways, close to home. We will see the changes first within the family, on social media, in the local pub. As we realize the possibilities that lie dormant, and begin to notice their impact upon our daily lives, so we cannot help but awaken to the possibilities on a global scale. We will understand how, with the right type of heart-centered asking, the answers come easily, and we will see that the Universe unfailingly responds no matter how apparently insignificant or grand the project. We will learn that happiness cannot possibly lie along paths which hold sorrow for others, so we will renounce them and choose another route. In seeking nothing solely for ourselves, we gain everything.

Our obsession with the self, in all its many fearful guises – self-seeking, self-serving, self-delusion, self-esteem, self-pity, self-interest, self-absorption, selfishness in general – and our lack of regard for others lies at the heart of the majority of our difficulties. If we are to evolve as a global community so we must learn to put others at the center of all that we choose for ourselves. In so doing we will find that we, too, are at the heart of everything.

We must learn to live together as brothers or perish together as fools.
– Martin Luther King Jr.

Choosing for the well-being of others does not mean renouncing our own needs. On the contrary, every act of self-care is radical. We cannot provide water for another if we ourselves do not have water. Nor does it mean sacrificing our uniqueness. There is not a musical work on the planet that can adequately describe the diversity of the human species. Not even if there were a million instruments, each capable of playing a thousand octaves. But just as in a piece of music, there will be times that there is discord, when we disagree and the discomfort of the clash will urge us to move towards something that feels more soothing. There will be other times when the introduction of a new element brings everything back into resolution, to the relief of beautiful harmony. We each contribute our own personal sound to the music of life. No one will see things in quite the same way that we do, each will view life through the filters of their own experiences. The extent to which we are able to express our distinctiveness, in collaboration with others who are also able to fully express theirs, is the extent to which we are truly free. It is the very essence of freedom.

The leaf has a very different form and texture to the branch, but they are both part of the same tree. Without the branch there would be no leaf, and without the leaf there would be no photosynthesis, and thus the tree would not live long. If one part suffers then all suffer. Better, then, for all to flourish. We all bring different gifts that are of benefit to a greater whole, we are all of service in our own way, and each of us is breathed in different rhythms by a life force far greater than any intellect can comprehend.

Our personal well-being is entirely dependent upon the well-being of the communities within which we are actively participating, whether that be a school or a village, a tennis club or a political party, a country, our planet or the cosmos itself. Not one of these communities exists in isolation. Each is nested within another. From the fungus that grows in the forest, to the man who labors hard to collect the rubbish for local government, each is a system within a system and has a role to play. Enable each to view things from their own perspective, to fully express their own unique voice, to unfold in their own manner and to live in peace. Live and let live without imposing. Ensure the respect of healthy boundaries, be allowing whenever it is reasonable to do so, but never forget the interdependence of all things.

The notion of the self-made man is nothing but a fallacy. We are made of the stuff of stars and the kind deeds of others. We breathe air that has filtered through the lungs of trees. We are molded by words of encouragement and chastisement. We are disciplined and trained like trees in a productive ornamental garden, shaped by the societies within which we live and the opinions of others. Those that thrive will not be the ones who fiercely battle to defend their differences, but those with open minds and open hearts who doggedly seek and develop what is held in common and who establish authentic connection.

Then you can care for all things.
– **Lao Tzu**

In African philosophy the concept of *Ubuntu* speaks to the sense of belonging and interconnection with others, to the very essence of being human.

We say a person is a person through other persons. I can't be human in isolation. I need you to be all you can be so that I can become me and all that I can be.
– **Desmond Mpilo Tutu**

The thread of humanity within each of us is inextricably bound together in a vast bundle of life. When we are concerned with the general welfare of that which is greater than the individual then we become generous, warmhearted and loving. We are compassionate, hospitable and we wisely share what we have. We lose all fear that someone might do better than us, because we understand the value that comes from enabling others to live to their full potential. The terror of failure fades into insignificance. We realize that when someone is oppressed then we all become smaller. We achieve that sense of connection that we all yearn for, a sense of purpose, of being a small part of something infinitely bigger.

Everyone is God speaking.
Why not be polite and
Listen to
Him?
– **Hafiz**

As we seek to identify, rather than compare, we find that no matter what our differences, our blood is all the same shade of red, and it is stirred by the same vital life force. As we look deeply into the hearts of others and love the world just as we would love ourselves, then we realize that we are not so very different after all. When we look at others we will only ever see ourselves reflected back and the way of love becomes the only way, the ultimate way.

There is nothing more lovable than myself in all directions.
– Udana Varga 5.18 – Buddhist Sacred Text

This is the way of the heart. Know that this is the way.

The secret method of inviting happiness through many blessings,
the spiritual medicine for all disease:

Just for today
Do not worry
Do not bear anger
Be grateful
Practice diligently, being true to your way and your being
Show compassion to yourself and others

Mornings and evenings repeat these words out loud and in your
heart
For the improvement of mind and body

– Usui Spiritual Healing Method, **Mikao Usui**

Bibliography

Abd-Ru-Shin (1995). *In the Light of Truth: The Grail Message Vols 1–3*. Gambier, Ohio: Grail Foundation Press.

Alchemy Realm (n.d.). "The Hara: center of balance" [online]. Available at: http://www.alchemyrealm.com/hara.htm [Accessed 13 June 2018].

Alexander, J. (2015). *The Best Lao Tzu Quotes (The Best Quotes Book 12)*, Kindle Edition. Crombie Jardine Publishing Limited.

Anon. (2018). Brainy quote [online]. "Charles Fillmore." Available at: https://www.brainyquote.com/quotes/keywords/childlike.html [Accessed 13 June 2018].

Bailey, A. (1993). *A Treatise on the Seven Rays*. New York: Lucis Publishing Co.

Bailey, A. (1995). *The seven rays of life*, 1st ed. New York: Lucis Publishing Co.

Barham, F. (2012). *The political works of Marcus Tullius Cicero, comprising his Treatise on the republic and his Treatise on the laws*. Ulan Press, p. 156.

Barley, A. (2018). "5 Rhythms" [online]. Adam Barley. Available at: http://www.adambarley.com/#5rhythms [Accessed 18 June 2018].

Berzin, A. (2003–18). "Letter to a Friend" [online]. Studybuddhism.com. Available at: https://studybuddhism.com/en/tibetan-buddhism/original-texts/sutra-texts/letter-to-a-friend [Accessed 19 August 2018].

Blakeslee, S. (1996). "Complex and Hidden Brain in Gut Makes Stomachaches and Butterflies" [online]. nytimes.com. Available at: http://www.nytimes.com/1996/01/23/science/complex-and-hidden-brain-in-gut-makes-stomachaches-and-butterflies.html [Accessed 18 June 2018].

Brennan, B. (1988). *Hands of Light: A Guide to Healing Through the Human Energy Field*. Bantam.

Broers, D. (2012). *Solar Revolution* [online video]. Gaia. Available at: https://www.gaia.com/video/solar-revolution [Accessed 18 June 2018].

Brown, B. (2013). *Brené Brown on empathy* [online video]. The RSA. Available at: https://www.youtube.com/watch?time_continue=95&v=1Evwgu369Jw [Accessed 20 June 2018].

Burke, G. (n.d.). "The Practice of Breath Meditation" [online]. Original Christianity and Original Yoga. Available at: https://ocoy.org/original-yoga/how-to-meditate/the-breath-of-life-the-practice-of-breath-meditation/practice-of-breath-meditation/ [Accessed 19 June 2018].

Campbell, T. (2017). *Physicist Tom Campbell: Virtual Reality, Simulation Theory, OBE's and Beyond. 1/2* [online video]. YouTube. Available at: https://www.youtube.com/watch?v=9dj5337UQmE&t=5438s+1.21 [Accessed 18 June 2018].

Carlyle, M. (2010). *How to Become a Money Magnet*. London: Hay House.

Carpenter, D. (2009). "The Vortex and the Path of Liberation: the Torus, the Vortex, and the Vacuum" [online]. Light-weaver. com. Available at: http://www.light-weaver.com/LW-old/vortex/1vortex.html [Accessed 18 June 2018].

Carrey, J. (1997). *The Oprah Winfrey Show* [TV program]. Harpo Studios. 17 February.

Carroll, L. (2017). "Kryon channelling: April 1 & 2 2017" [MP3]. Regina, SK, Canada. Available at: http://audio.kryon.com/en/Regina-notready-17.mp3 [Accessed 15 June 2018].

Carroll, L. (2017). "Kryon channelling: 1 July 2017" [MP3]. Laguna Hills, CA. Available at: http://audio.kryon.com/en/Saturday-laguna-17.mp3.

Cernuskova, V.; Kovacs, J. and Plátová, J. (2017). *Clement's Biblical Exegesis: Proceedings of the Second Colloquium on Clement of Alexandria (Olomouc, May 29–31, 2014)*. Leiden; Boston: Brill, p. 286.

Chaimbentorah.com (2015). "Word Study – Bad Breath לֹא

רח." Available at: http://www.chaimbentorah.com/2018/11/hebrew-word-study-bad-breath/ [Accessed 13 June 2018].

Chang, L. (2006). *Wisdom for the Soul: Five Millennia of Prescriptions for Spiritual Healing*. Washington, DC: Gnosophia Publishers.

Chernoff, A. (2014). "10 Truths You Will Learn Before You Find Happiness" [online]. Marc and Angel Hack Life. Available at: http://www.marcandangel.com/2013/10/15/10-truths-you-will-learn-before-you-find-happiness/ [Accessed 15 June 2018].

Chödrön, P. (2006). *Practicing Peace*. Boston, MA: Shambhala, p. 59.

Chopra, D. (1994). *The Seven Spiritual Laws of Success*. San Rafael, CA: New World Library, p. 9.

Clayton, M.; Sager, R. and Will, U. (2004). *In time with the music: the concept of entrainment and its significance for ethnomusicology* [e-book]. Available at: http://oro.open.ac.uk/2661/1/InTimeWithTheMusic.pdf [Accessed 18 June 2018].

Covey, S. (2004). *The 7 Habits of Highly Effective People*. New York: Free Press.

Crockett, C. (2018). "What is a coronal mass ejection?" [online] EarthSky.org. Available at: http://earthsky.org/space/what-are-coronal-mass-ejections [Accessed 18 June 2018].

Cultivate Calm Yoga (2018). "Breathe your way to better health – part 1" [blog]. Brisbane: Cultivatecalmyoga.com.au. Available at: http://cultivatecalmyoga.com.au/breathe-your-way-to-better-health-part-1/ [Accessed 15 June 2018].

Currivan, J. (2018). "The Emergence of Conscious Evolution: Jude Currivan" [online]. YouTube. Available at: https://www.youtube.com/watch?v=zQ6IGEpq2kg [Accessed 16 August 2018].

Currivan, J. and Laszlo, E. (2017). *The Cosmic Hologram: In-formation at the Center of Creation*. Rochester, VT: Inner Traditions.

D'Ambrose, C. (2003). "Frequency Range of Human Hearing." The Physics Factbook – an encyclopedia of scientific essays [online].

Hypertextbook.com. Available at: https://hypertextbook.com/facts/2003/ChrisDAmbrose.shtml [Accessed 19 June 2018].

Dashu, M. (2009). "The Pythias" excerpted from *Secret History of the Witches* [e-book]. Available at: http://www.suppressedhistories.net/secrethistory/Pythia.pdf [Accessed 15 June 2018].

Deacon, J. (2010). "Mantra, Jumon, & Kotodama" [online]. James Deacon's Reiki pages – aetw.org. Available at: http://www.aetw.org/reiki_mantra_jumon_kotodama.html [Accessed 15 June 2018].

Disney, A. (2017). "Heiress Abigail Disney Opposes GOP Tax Bill" [online]. NowThis. Available at: https://nowthisnews.com/videos/politics/heiress-abigail-disney-opposes-gop-tax-bill [Accessed 21 August 2018].

Dobson, T.; Moss, R. and Watson, J. (1993). *It's a Lot like Dancing: An Aikido Journey..* Berkeley, CA: Frog, p. 165.

Doreal, M. (1994). *The Emerald Tablets of Thoth-the-Atlantean*, 2nd ed. Lanham: Source Books Inc.

Dove, L. (2018). "How many atoms are in a person?" [online]. HowStuffWorks. Available at: https://science.howstuffworks.com/atoms-in-person.htm [Accessed 19 June 2018].

Dürckheim, K. (2004). *Hara: The Vital Center of Man*, 4th edition. Rochester, VT: Inner Traditions.

Dyer, W. (2008). *Change Your Thoughts – Change Your Life: Living the Wisdom of the Tao*. Carlsbad, CA: Hay House, Inc.

Dyer, W. (2018). *5 Lessons To Live By – Dr. Wayne Dyer (Truly Inspiring)*. [online] YouTube. Available at: https://www.youtube.com/watch?v=dOkNkcZ_THA [Accessed 19 August 2018].

En.wikipedia.org (2018). "Logos" [online]. Available at: https://en.wikipedia.org/wiki/Logos [Accessed 15 June 2018].

En.wikipedia.org (2018). "Mei (given name)" [online]. Available at: https://en.wikipedia.org/wiki/Mei_(given_name) [Accessed 15 June 2018].

En.wikipedia.org (2018). "Spirit" [online]. Available at: https://en.wikipedia.org/wiki/Spirit [Accessed 13 June 2018].

En.wikiquote.org (2018). "Morihei Ueshiba." Wikiquote [online]. Available at: https://en.wikiquote.org/wiki/Morihei_Ueshiba [Accessed 19 June 2018].

Esotericonline.net (2012). "Introduction to Breath Meditation" [online]. Available at: http://www.esotericonline.net/group/the-meditation-room/forum/topics/introduction-to-breath-meditation [Accessed 13 June 2018].

Evolution Television (2013). *Cancer Cured in 3 Minutes – Awesome Presentation by Gregg Braden* [online video]. Available at: https://www.youtube.com/watch?v=VLPahLakP_Q [Accessed 13 June 2018].

Facebook.com (2013). "Awakening the Hara Consciousness" [online]. The Hara: Sacred Center. Available at: https://www.facebook.com/HaraConsciousness/posts/543426892409692 [Accessed 13 June 2018].

Fillmore, C. (2012). *Prosperity: Spiritual Secrets to an Abundant Life*. Kansas City, MO: Dover Publications, p. 82.

Firstpeople.us (n.d.). "First people: words of wisdom index – Black Elk" [online]. Available at: http://www.firstpeople.us/FP-Html-Wisdom/BlackElk.html [Accessed 19 June 2018].

Forrest, S. (2012). *The Inner Sky*. Borrego Springs, CA: Seven Paws Press.

Gibbon, E. (1999). *The Decline and Fall of the Roman Empire*. Ware: Wordsworth Editions Ltd, p. 1036.

Gnosis.org (n.d.). "The Corpus Hermeticum and Hermetic Tradition," The Gnostic Society Library [online]. Available at: http://gnosis.org/library/hermet.htm#CH [Accessed 19 August 2018].

Hale, T. (2018). "Mountaineers Who Suffer Moments Of Psychosis Are Not Just Experiencing Altitude Sickness" [online]. IFLScience. Available at: http://www.iflscience.com/brain/mountaineers-who-suffer-moments-of-psychosis-are-not-just-experiencing-altitude-sickness/ [Accessed 13 June 2018].

Hall, M. (2011). *The Secret Teachings of All Ages*. US: Pacific Publishing Studio.

HeartMath® Institute (2018). "Global Coherence Research – The Science of Interconnectivity" [online]. Available at: https://www.heartmath.org/research/global-coherence/ [Accessed 18 June 2018].

Hicks, E. and Hicks, J. (2013). "Got 68 Seconds? That's all it takes to get your wish!" [online]. Healyourlife.com, Hay House Inc. Available at: https://www.healyourlife.com/got-68-seconds [Accessed 15 June 2018].

Hicks, E. and Hicks, J. (2004). *Ask and it is given*. Carlsbad, CA: Hay House Inc.

Higher Perspective (2015). "23 Nikola Tesla Quotes That Will Electrify Your Life" [online]. Available at: http://www.higherperspectives.com/nikola-tesla-quotes-1406167140.html [Accessed 18 June 2018].

Hill, N. (2008). *Think and Grow Rich*. NY: Jeremy P. Tarcher/Penguin, p. 155.

Holliwell, R. (2004). *Working With the Law: 11 Truth Principles for Successful Living*. Camarillo, CA: DeVorss Publications.

Khan, H. (1996). *The Mysticism of Sound and Music: The Sufi Teaching of Hazrat Inayat Khan*. Boston, MA: Shambhala, pp. 24, 27, 170, 263, 265, 269.

Kim, T. (1991). *Seven Steps to Inner Power*. San Rafael, CA: New World Library.

Kirpalsingh.org (n.d.). *The Ambrosial Hour* [e-book]. Available at: http://kirpalsingh.org/Booklets/Ambrosial_Hour.pdf [Accessed 13 June 2018].

Lao Tzu (n.d.). "Lao Tzu – Tao Te Ching (Stephen Mitchell Translation)." [online] Genius. Available at: https://genius.com/Lao-tzu-tao-te-ching-stephen-mitchell-translation-annotated [Accessed 18 August 2018].

Lao Tzu (n.d.). "Tao Te Ching by Lao Tzu Chapter Forty-Four."

[online] Thetaoteching.com. Available at: http://thetaoteching. com/taoteching44.html [Accessed 18 August 2018].

Lao Tzu, DaltheJigsaw (2011). "When I let go of what I am, I become what I might be – Lao Tzu." [online] NewBuddhist. Available at: http://newbuddhist.com/discussion/12415/ when-i-let-go-of-what-i-am-i-become-what-i-might-be-lao-tzu [Accessed 18 August 2018].

Lao Tzu; Feng, G.; English, J.; Lippe, T. and Needleman, J. (2011). *Tao Te Ching – Lao Tsu*. US: Vintage, verses 1, 29, 33, 57.

Lee, B.; McDougall, D. and Silliphant, S. (1971). *Longstreet*, "The Way of the Intercepting Fist" [TV program]. US: ABC, 16 September.

Lipton, B. (2009). *The Biology of Belief*. Carlsbad, CA: Hay House.

Loria, K. (2018). "Mountain climbers experience mysterious hallucinations that doctors are calling a new condition." [online] Business Insider France. Available at: http://www. businessinsider.fr/us/high-altitude-climbers-psychosis-hallucinations-2018-1 [Accessed 13 June 2018].

Lübeck, W.; Petter, F.; Rand, W. and Grimm, C. (2001). *The Spirit of Reiki*. Twin Lakes, WI: Lotus Press.

Magic Point (2012–2018). "Terra, the torus" [online]. Available at: http://www.magic-point.org/terra-the-torus/ [Accessed 13 June 2018].

Marchand, P. (2006). *The Yoga of the Nine Emotions: The Tantric Practice of Rasa Sadhana Based on the teachings of Harish Johari*. Rochester, VT: Destiny Books.

Martel, J. (2015). *The Complete Dictionary of Ailments and Diseases*. Québec: Les Editions ATMA Internationales.

Matsuura, P. (1974). "Mrs. Takata and Reiki Power." *Honolulu Advertiser* [online]. Reiki.org. Available at: http://www.reiki. org/reikinews/reikin7.html [Accessed 19 June 2018].

McTaggart, L. (2003). *The Field*. London: Element.

Medium (n.d.). "Transcendental Hearing: Important Points About Inner Sound Meditation Practice" [online]. Available at: https://medium.com/sant-mat-meditation-and-spirituality/transcendental-hearing-important-points-about-inner-sound-meditation-practice-a4446e592b27 [Accessed 21 August 2018].

Mooji (2017). *Stop! And Be Like the Sky* [video]. Available at: https://www.youtube.com/watch?v=9NCPCw1kI_U [Accessed 20 June 2018].

Morris, S. (2010). "Achieving collective coherence" [PDF]. *Alternative Therapies*, Jul/Aug 2010. Vol. 16. No. 4. Available at: https://www.heartmath.org/assets/uploads/2015/01/achieving-collective-coherence.pdf [Accessed 18 June 2018].

Murdoch, A. (2006). *Breathe* [MP3]. Blue Mind Music.

Nave, R. (n.d.). "Axial tilt is critical for life" [online]. Available at: http://hyperphysics.phy-astr.gsu.edu/hbase/Astro/orbtilt.html [Accessed 13 June 2018].

New Scientist (1996). "The last word" [online]. Available at: https://www.newscientist.com/article/mg15020308-500-the-last-word/ [Accessed 13 June 2018].

Nhất Hạnh, T. (1999). *The Heart of the Buddha's Teaching: Transforming Suffering into Peace, Joy, and Liberation*. NY: Harmony Books, p. 154.

Ni, M. (1995). *The Yellow Emperor's Classic of Medicine*. Boston, MA: Shambhala.

Nizer, L. (2012). *My Life in Court*. Eastford, CT: Martino Fine Books.

Osho (n.d.). "Tantric Transformation: Intelligence is Meditation" [online]. Osho Online Library. Available at: http://www.osho.com/iosho/library/read-book/online-library-senses-tantra-body-8a58412c-db1?p=d7c135cfa481cb4e0fedd0cd780e0981 [Accessed 20 June 2018].

Palmer, P. (2017). *The Courage to Teach: Exploring the Inner Landscape of a Teacher's Life*, 20th ed. Hoboken, NJ: Jossey-Bass, p. 58.

Pennington, J. (2011). "The Brain Waves of Reiki" [online]. International House of Reiki. Available at: http://www.ihreiki.

com/blog/article/the_brain_waves_of_reiki [Accessed 18 June 2018].

Pluto.space.swri.edu (n.d.). "Plasma: the Fourth State of Matter" [online]. Available at: http://pluto.space.swri.edu/image/glossary/plasma.html [Accessed 18 June 2018].

Poe, E. (2016). *The Poetic Principle*. CreateSpace Independent Publishing Platform, p. 12.

Profound Talks (2017). *Rupert Spira (September 8, 2017) – Explaining the NOW Very Clearly* [online]. Available at: https://www.youtube.com/watch?v=3yuuBLztdhM&t=103s [Accessed 20 September 2018].

Qi Healers Without Borders (2011). "Cultivating Qi Energy in the Hara & Its Energetic Pathways" [online]. Available at: http://www.qiwithoutborders.org/hara.html [Accessed 13 June 2018].

Reid, J. (n.d.). "Sound Gives Birth To Light: How Our Songs And Words Reach The Stars" [PDF]. Available at: http://www.cymascope.com [Accessed 18 June 2018].

Rennebarth, K. (n.d.). "The hara – shiatsu and other natural health healing techniques" [online]. Available at: http://www.shiatsuman.com/the_hara.html [Accessed 13 June 2018].

Ricard, M. (2015). *Happiness*. London: Atlantic Books.

Roberson, S. (2016). *The Money Shift (Manifesting Abundance Book 1)* [online]. Amazon.

Ruiz, M. (1997). *The Four Agreements: A Practical Guide to Personal Freedom (A Toltec Wisdom Book)*. San Rafael, CA: Amber-Allen Publishing.

Sadhguru (2012). *Impact Of Solar Flares On Human Consciousness, Sadhguru* [online]. YouTube. Available at: https://www.youtube.com/watch?v=hCCNpPNigVc [Accessed 18 June 2018].

Saraswati, S. (2007–18). "Pranayama: The Breath of Life – Sri Swami Satchidananda" [online]. Sri Swami Satchidananda. Available at: http://swamisatchidananda.org/pranayama-breath-life/ [Accessed 17 August 2018].

Schirber, M. (2005). "Ice Ages Blamed on Tilted Earth" [online]. Available at: https://www.livescience.com/6937-ice-ages-blamed-tilted-earth.html [Accessed 13 June 2018].

Schucman, H. (2009). *A Course In Miracles: Original Edition Text.* Omaha, NE: Course in Miracles Society, pp. 155, 277.

Science Learning Hub (2007). "Does blood have magnetic properties?" [online]. Available at: https://www.sciencelearn.org.nz/resources/1010-does-blood-have-magnetic-properties [Accessed 13 June 2018].

Selig, P. (2010). *I Am the Word: A Guide to the Consciousness of Man's Self in a Transitioning Time.* New York: Jeremy P. Tarcher/Penguin.

Serrano, R. (2011). *Meditation and Qigong Mastery.* North Vancouver, Canada: Holisticwebs.com, p. 73.

Seth; Roberts, J. and Butts, R. (1994). *The Nature of Personal Reality.* San Rafael, CA: New World Library.

Shakespeare, W. and Watts, C. (2004). *The Tempest.* Ware: Wordsworth Editions Limited, p. 16.

Shakti Caterina Maggi (n.d.). "Shakti" [online]. Shakti Caterina Maggi. Available at: http://www.shakticaterinamaggi.com/shakti/ [Accessed 20 August 2018].

Shankar, HH Sri Sri Ravi (2013). *Love is not an Emotion: It is your very existence.* US: Sri Sri Publication.

Shaw, GB (1988). *Back to Methuselah: A Metabiological Pentateuch.* London: Penguin Books, p. 213.

Siegel, D. (2016). *Nature, Wellbeing, Love & Spirit: The Deep Mystery of Humanity* [online video]. Sages & Scientists Symposium. Available at: https://www.facebook.com/DeepakChopra/videos/10153911981515665/ [Accessed 19 June 2018].

Singleton, T. (2015). "No words... only love" [online]. Tigmonk. Available at: https://tigmonk.com/no-wordsonly-love/ [Accessed 20 June 2018].

Sivananda (2000). *Autobiography of Swami Sivananda* [online].

Dlshq.org. Available at: http://www.dlshq.org/download/autobio.htm [Accessed 20 August 2018].

Sivertsen, L. (2016). "Guru Singh: Buried Treasures Revealed." Beautiful Writers Podcast. Available at: https://itunes.apple.com/de/podcast/beautiful-writers-podcast/id1047012231?l=en&mt=2 [Accessed 13 June 2018].

Sound Healing Resource (2007). *The Shape of Sound featuring John Stuart Reid*: excerpt from 2006 International Sound Healing Conference in Santa Fe [online]. Available at: https://www.youtube.com/watch?v=GlkIxpuF43o [Accessed 18 June 2018].

Steiner, R. (1998). "Lecture: The Etherisation of the Blood," delivered in Basle, 1911 [online]. Wn.rsarchive.org. Available at: https://wn.rsarchive.org/Lectures/19111001p01.html [Accessed 19 June 2018].

Stenudd, S. (n.d.). *Ki Energy: The Life Force of the Far East* [e-book]. Available at: http://www.stenudd.com/aikido/ki-energy.htm [Accessed 13 June 2018].

Stiene, F. (2014). "Heart/Mind and Hands on Healing" [blog]. International House of Reiki.com. Available at: http://www.ihreiki.com/blog/article/heart_mind_and_hands_on_healing [Accessed 13 June 2018].

Stiene, F. (2017). *What is Reiki?* Frans Stiene, International House of Reiki. International Reiki conference Sydney 2015 [video]. Meditation & Healing House. Available at: https://www.youtube.com/watch?v=b4WHdqX_xqU [Accessed 19 June 2018].

Tagore, R. (2016). *Stray Birds* (1916) by Rabindranath Tagore [online]. En.wikisource.org. Available at: https://en.wikisource.org/wiki/Stray_Birds [Accessed 20 August 2018].

Tesla, N. (1892). "Experiments with alternate currents of high potential and high frequency" [online]. Open Tesla Research. Lecture delivered before the Institution of Electrical Engineers, London. Available at: https://teslaresearch.jimdo.com/lectures-of-nikola-tesla/experiments-with-alternate-currents-of-high-potential-and-high-frequency-a-lecture-delivered-before-the-iee-london-february-1892/ [Accessed 19 June 2018].

Tesla, N. (2018). "The Problem of Increasing Human Energy With Special Reference to the Harnessing of the Sun's Energy" by Nikola Tesla, *Century Magazine*, June 1900, pp. 175–211. [online] Tesla Universe. Available at: https://teslauniverse. com/nikola-tesla/articles/problem-increasing-human-energy [Accessed 20 August 2018].

Tessenow, H. and Unschuld, P. (2011). *Huang Di Nei Jing Su Wen: An Annotated Translation of Huang Di's Inner Classic – Basic Questions, 2 Volumes*, Volumes of the *Huang Di nei jing su wen* Project. Berkeley and Los Angeles: University of California Press, p. 594.

The Cosmometry Project (n.d.). "The Torus – Dynamic Flow Process" [online]. Available at: http://cosmometry.net/the-torus---dynamic-flow-process [Accessed 13 June 2018].

The Editors of Encyclopaedia Britannica, Duignan, B. and Sampaolo, M. (1998). "Logos: Philosophy and Theology" [online]. *Encyclopaedia Britannica*. Available at: https://www. britannica.com/topic/logos [Accessed 20 September 2018].

The Threshold Society (n.d.). "Poems of Rumi tr. by Coleman Barks" [online]. Available at: https://sufism.org/origins/ rumi/rumi-excerpts/poems-of-rumi-tr-by-coleman-barks-published-by-threshold-books-2 [Accessed 13 June 2018].

Three Initiates (2018). *The Kybalion: Hermetic Philosophy, Centenary Edition*. NY: Penguin Publishing Group.

Thrive Movement (2011–2018). "The Code/Fundamental Pattern" [online]. Available at: http://www.thrivemovement.com/the_ code-fundamental_pattern [Accessed 13 June 2018].

Tolle, E. (2009). *A New Earth: Awakening to Your Life's Purpose*. Camberwell, VIC: Penguin.

Tolle, E. (2004). *The Power of Now*. Vancouver: Namaste Publishing.

Venkataramiah, M. (2013). *Talks with Sri Ramana Maharshi*, 1st ed. Tamil Nadu: VS Ramanan, p. 309.

Vivekananda (2009). *Personality development*, 2nd ed. Uttarakhand: Advaita Ashram.

Von Hochheim, E. (2018). A quote by Meister Eckhart [online]. Goodreads.com. Available at: https://www.goodreads.com/quotes/582851-theologians-may-quarrel-but-the-mystics-of-the-world-speak [Accessed 15 August 2018].

Walsch, N. (1997). *Conversations with God*. London: Hodder and Stoughton.

West, J. (2012). "Gnosticism and the Gospel of John: Gnostic enigmas in the Gospel of John" [online]. Available at: https://ogdoas.wordpress.com/category/gnosticism-and-the-gospel-of-john/ [Accessed 15 June 2018].

White Magic Way (2016). "The Bovis Biometer" [online]. Available at: http://whitemagicway.com/bovisbiometer.html [Accessed 18 June 2018].

Williams, M. (2016). "What is Earth's Axial Tilt?" [online]. Available at: https://www.universetoday.com/47176/earths-axis/ [Accessed 13 June 2018].

Wong, E. (2015). *Being Taoist: Wisdom for Living a Balanced Life*. Boulder, CO: Shambhala Publications Inc.

Yogananda, P. (1982). *Man's Eternal Quest: Collected Talks and Essays, Volume 1*, 2nd ed. Los Angeles, CA: Self-Realization Fellowship, p. 143.

Yusuf, H. (2004). *Purification of the Heart: Signs, Symptoms and Cures of the Spiritual Diseases of the Heart*. Bridgeview, IL: Starlatch.

Note from the Author

Thank you for purchasing *Ancient Teachings for Modern Times*. If it has brought you even a fraction of the insight and peace of mind that I gleaned while I was writing it, then my time has been well spent. I hope you enjoyed it, return to it often and share it with your friends and loved ones. We all need a gentle reminder from time to time.

If you are inspired by the principles I've shared in this book and would like to learn more, you can connect with me on Facebook or at one of the many courses and workshops I run, the details of which you can find at: www.petamorton.com.

BOOKS

O-BOOKS

SPIRITUALITY

O is a symbol of the world, of oneness and unity; this eye represents knowledge and insight. We publish titles on general spirituality and living a spiritual life. We aim to inform and help you on your own journey in this life.
If you have enjoyed this book, why not tell other readers by posting a review on your preferred book site?

Recent bestsellers from O-Books are:

Heart of Tantric Sex
Diana Richardson
Revealing Eastern secrets of deep love and intimacy to Western
couples.
Paperback: 978-1-90381-637-0 ebook: 978-1-84694-637-0

Crystal Prescriptions
The A-Z guide to over 1,200 symptoms and the stones that heal
them
Judy Hall
The first in the popular series of six books, this handy little
guide is packed as tight as a pill-bottle with crystal remedies for
ailments.
Paperback: 978-1-90504-740-6 ebook: 978-1-84694-629-5

Take Me To Truth
Undoing the Ego
Nouk Sanchez, Tomas Vieira
The best-selling step-by-step book on shedding the Ego, using the
teachings of *A Course In Miracles*.
Paperback: 978-1-84694-050-7 ebook: 978-1-84694-654-7

The 7 Myths about Love...Actually!
The journey from your HEAD to the HEART of your SOUL
Mike George
Smashes all the myths about LOVE.
Paperback: 978-1-84694-288-4 ebook: 978-1-84694-682-0

Your Simple Path
Find Happiness in every step
Ian Tucker
A guide to helping us reconnect with what is really important in our lives.
Paperback: 978-1-78279-349-6 ebook: 978-1-78279-348-9

365 Days of Wisdom
Daily Messages To Inspire You Through The Year
Dadi Janki
Daily messages which cool the mind, warm the heart and guide you along your journey.
Paperback: 978-1-84694-863-3 ebook: 978-1-84694-864-0

Body of Wisdom
Women's Spiritual Power and How it Serves
Hilary Hart
Bringing together the dreams and experiences of women across the world with today's most visionary spiritual teachers.
Paperback: 978-1-78099-696-7 ebook: 978-1-78099-695-0

Dying to Be Free
From Enforced Secrecy to Near Death to True Transformation
Hannah Robinson
After an unexpected accident and near-death experience, Hannah Robinson found herself radically transforming her life, while a remarkable new insight altered her relationship with her father, a practising Catholic priest.
Paperback: 978-1-78535-254-6 ebook: 978-1-78535-255-3

The Ecology of the Soul
A Manual of Peace, Power and Personal Growth for Real People
in the Real World
Aidan Walker
Balance your own inner Ecology of the Soul to regain your
natural state of peace, power and wellbeing.
Paperback: 978-1-78279-850-7 ebook: 978-1-78279-849-1

Not I, Not other than I
The Life and Teachings of Russel Williams
Steve Taylor, Russel Williams
The miraculous life and inspiring teachings of one of the World's
greatest living Sages.
Paperback: 978-1-78279-729-6 ebook: 978-1-78279-728-9

On the Other Side of Love
A woman's unconventional journey towards wisdom
Muriel Maufroy
When life has lost all meaning, what do you do?
Paperback: 978-1-78535-281-2 ebook: 978-1-78535-282-9

Practicing A Course In Miracles
A translation of the Workbook in plain language, with
mentor's notes
Elizabeth A. Cronkhite
The practical second and third volumes of The Plain-Language
A Course In Miracles.
Paperback: 978-1-84694-403-1 ebook: 978-1-78099-072-9

Quantum Bliss
The Quantum Mechanics of Happiness, Abundance, and Health
George S. Mentz
Quantum Bliss is the breakthrough summary of success and
spirituality secrets that customers have been waiting for.
Paperback: 978-1-78535-203-4 ebook: 978-1-78535-204-1

The Upside Down Mountain
Mags MacKean
A must-read for anyone weary of chasing success and happiness
– one woman's inspirational journey swapping the uphill slog for
the downhill slope.
Paperback: 978-1-78535-171-6 ebook: 978-1-78535-172-3

Your Personal Tuning Fork
The Endocrine System
Deborah Bates
Discover your body's health secret, the endocrine system, and
'twang' your way to sustainable health!
Paperback: 978-1-84694-503-8 ebook: 978-1-78099-697-4

Readers of ebooks can buy or view any of these bestsellers by clicking on the live link in the title. Most titles are published in paperback and as an ebook. Paperbacks are available in traditional bookshops. Both print and ebook formats are available online.

Find more titles and sign up to our readers' newsletter at http://www.johnhuntpublishing.com/mind-body-spirit

Follow us on Facebook at https://www.facebook.com/OBooks/ and Twitter at https://twitter.com/obooks